JOHN MASEFIELD

LITERATURE AND LIFE:
BRITISH WRITERS

Complete list of titles in the series available from the
publisher on request.

JOHN MASEFIELD

June Dwyer

UNGAR • NEW YORK

1987

The Ungar Publishing Company
370 Lexington Avenue, New York, NY 10017

Copyright © 1987 by The Ungar Publishing Company

Printed in the United States of America

Library of Congress Cataloging-in-Publication Data

Dwyer, June.
  John Masefield.

  (Literature and life. British writers)
  Bibliography: p.
  Includes index.
  1. Masefield, John, 1878–1967—Criticism and
interpretation. I. Title. II. Series.
PR6025.A77Z63   1987   818'.91209   87-5883
ISBN 0-8044-2164-1

Contents

Acknowledgments

Masefield admirers are an outgoing and generous group of people. Dr. Corliss Lamont, Miss Audrey Napier-Smith ("Reyna"), Mr. Geoffrey Handley-Taylor, and Dr. Fraser Drew all volunteered scholarly information and personal reminiscences about Masefield to me for which I am very grateful. Constance Babington Smith's excellent biography of the poet provided me with a great deal of useful information throughout my study. Her bibliography of Masefield's enormous oeuvre was invaluable.

I would also like to thank the staff of the Berg Collection of the New York Public Library where Masefield's letters to Elizabeth Robins are housed. To Frank Walker, head librarian of New York University's Fales Collection, I owe special gratitude. He was both patient and helpful as I read through the difficult-to-find Masefield works and personal papers in that excellent rare book library.

Closer to home, my colleague, poet John Fandel, lent me his poet's eye and his personal encouragement during this project. I found both most welcome. Finally, my greatest debt is to my colleague Robert Kiernan for his expert advice and his patient and incisive reading of the manuscript.

All of these people have made my Masefield project a most enjoyable one. Any errors in this work are my own, and I regret them.

Chronology

June 1, 1878	John Masefield born in Ledbury, England.
Jan. 1885	Mother dies.
1890	William and Kate Masefield become guardians.
1891	Father dies.
Sept. 1891–Mar. 1894	School on HMS *Conway*.
Apr.–Aug. 1894	*Gilcruix* voyage.
Oct. 1894	Returns to England a DBS.
Mar. 1895	Fails to report to ship in New York.
Mar. 1895–summer 1895	Wanders around northeast US.
Sept. 1895–July 1897	Works at Smith's Carpet Mill.
July 1897	Returns to England.
1900	Meets Yeats.
1901	Leaves bank job for free-lance writing.

1902	*Salt-Water Ballads* published.
1903	Marriage to Constance Cromme-lin.
1904	Judith Masefield born.
1908	*Captain Margaret* published.
1909	*The Tragedy of Nan and Other Plays.*
1909–10	Correspondence with Elizabeth Robins.
1910	Lewis Masefield born.
1911	*The Street of Today* published.
1911	*The Everlasting Mercy* published.
1913	Publishes *Dauber*.
1915–18	War service in France, propaganda trip to America, visit to Gallipoli.
1916	Meets Florence Lamont.
1916–52	Correspondence with Florence Lamont.
1916	*Sonnets* published.

1960   Constance Masefield dies.

May 12, 1967   John Masefield dies.

1

•••

Biography

When he was thirty-one, John Masefield privately referred to his past as "squalid," but he hastened to add, "Don't think my life has been unhappy. My life has been a glorious miracle."[1] So in many ways it was. Masefield never exploited the rags-to-riches quality of his story, for his early life embarrassed him, as did some of his early behavior. After he was named Poet Laureate of England in 1930 and public interest in his life intensified, he masked the turbulence of his youth with low-keyed fragments of autobiography. The first full-scale account of his life, Constance Babington Smith's *John Masefield: A Life*, appeared eleven years after the poet's death. Smith retells Masefield's difficulties with understanding and grace, but she uncovered many episodes that Masefield had done his best to bury. As a result, we see him not as he wished, but more as he really was.

Masefield was born in Ledbury, Herefordshire on June 1, 1878, the third of six children. More than once in his later writings, he likened this early existence to life in paradise. His first six and a half years were spent in what appears to have been a Wordsworthian communion with nature. The happiness and stability of this early period were followed by fifteen years of difficulty and sadness that put a great strain on his overly sensitive nature.

Masefield's expulsion from his paradise came in January 1885 when his mother, Caroline Masefield, died of double pneumonia only a few weeks after having given birth to her sixth child. Financial reverses and the death of two grandparents the following year put further strains on the family. Edward Masefield, the poet's solicitor father, never recovered from these shocks, and, according to his son, "slowly sank into insanity."[2]

The children were looked after by a governess who was despised by them all; Masefield admitted to once stabbing her with a fork. He was not much happier with his life at Warwick School where he matriculated as a boarding student at the age of ten. "I was too young," he commented in later years, adding, "I tried to kill myself once by eating laurel leaves but only gave myself a horrible headache. Once I ran away, and was brought back by a policeman and flogged."[3] Later Masefield began to enjoy himself at Warwick but left early in 1890 when his father's condition worsened to the point where he had to be hospitalized.

Even before Edward Masefield's death in 1891, his six children needed a guardian. The job fell to his brother and sister-in-law, William and Kate Masefield, who had no surviving children of their own. Kate preferred the two youngest Masefields and was particularly hard on John who read too much for her liking. "I hated that woman," he admitted privately. She decided he was "a dangerous young Turk and should go to sea."[4] For the next two and a half years, Masefield went to school and learned seamanship aboard the HMS *Conway*, an instructional ship moored in the Liverpool harbor. It was neither an easy nor a genteel life, especially during the first term when Masefield was a "new chum." Nevertheless, he fit in well enough and developed a love for sailing ships and an admiration for at least some of the hardy men who lived on them. Masefield was not an outstanding student—mathematics was particularly difficult for him—but he did win an essay prize during his second year for "Proficiency in Writing, Spelling and Composition."[5] All during this time on the *Conway*, he continued the reading that his aunt had hoped shipboard life would curb.

Upon graduation, Masefield joined the sailing ship HMS *Gilcruix* as an apprentice, and in April 1894 he began his first and only sea voyage as a British sailor. The trip ended for him at Iquique, Chile, where he was put ashore suffering from sunstroke and apparently a nervous breakdown.[6] He was formally dismissed from the ship's crew, hospitalized for a time in Valparaiso, and then sent home by steamer a DBS—Distressed British Seaman.

Many factors contributed to his breakdown. In spite of his love for the sea and for sailing ships, Masefield was not a good sailor. He was seasick soon after the *Gilcruix* left England and continued to suffer bouts of seasickness throughout the voyage. In addition, Masefield was not at home with his fellow seamen; he made some friends, but others saw him as a "damned innocent" and an "odd fish."[7] The sailors were a brutal, blasphemous, and intolerant lot. His portrait of the gentle artist-seaman in the narrative poem *Dauber* (1913) is certainly drawn from his own unpleasant treatment on the *Gilcruix*. The seasickness and the loneliness were intensified by the difficulty of the voyage itself. The ship was trapped in an ice storm for thirty-two days around Cape Horn. Masefield's journal of the ship's progress breaks off at the beginning of this period. He may well have been too busy, too wet, and too cold to continue, but the project may also have been abandoned owing to the writer's growing instability.

Whatever the causes of his illness, Masefield returned home shaken and still unwell to be jeered at by his Aunt Kate for his failure. She quickly enlisted him on another ship, the *Bidston Hill*, which he was to meet in New York. He glumly took a steamer back across the Atlantic, feeling no romance or respect for the sailor's life. "The sea seemed to have me in her grip," he wrote. "I was to pass my life beating other men's ships to port. That was to be 'life' for me. The docks, and sailor town, and all the damning and the heaving."[8] Whether moved by fear or wisdom, or an equal measure of both, he never reported to his ship in New York. "I deserted my ship," he admitted later in a letter, "and cut myself adrift from her, and from my home. I was going to be a writer, come what might."[9]

Masefield was indeed adrift in America; at the age of seventeen, he became a tramp, doing odd jobs and wandering about the countryside while private detectives employed by his uncle searched for him without success. In a few months, he found himself in New York City again, working as a bar boy at the Columbian Hotel in Greenwich Village. From this seedy establishment he moved on to more respectable employment at the Alexander Smith and Sons' Carpet Mill in Yonkers. He remained there for two years. During this period of relative stability, Masefield read and wrote a great deal, but he also considered becoming a doctor. A young friend wrote on his behalf to the Masefield family explaining the circumstances and requesting some financial support for the project; but they refused.

With this door closed, Masefield continued to write and to work at the mill, but his health was poor. The early stages of tuberculosis had set in, and he was depressed over the collapse of his medical-school prospects. In the summer of 1897, after a dispute with his employer, Masefield resigned from his job and returned home. The young poet burned a large basketful of his writings, secured sea passage through his *Conway* connections, and sailed for England with a wealth of experience already behind him. He was barely nineteen. In later life he would look back benignly on his job at the Yonkers mill, but in 1900 Masefield privately termed his stay in America "a seclusion . . . among the looms of Yonkers, a seclusion due to my hatred of Americans."[10]

Life was kinder to him upon his return to England; a job

in a small business firm, followed by one in a bank, gave him a stable income and time to recover both his health and his self-esteem. The year 1899 brought an acceptance notice for one of his poems in *Outlook*, a literary and political journal. Tensions with his family relaxed somewhat, and Masefield drew close to his youngest sister Nora, who was then in her teens.

By the turn of the century, Masefield's literary life had begun in earnest; he met the poet William Butler Yeats in 1900 and was often present at his Monday-night gatherings. Through Yeats he came to know other prominent literary figures, among them the scholar and poet Lawrence Binyon and the Irish playwright John Synge. In 1901 Masefield left his bank job for the world of free-lance writing. He was twenty-three at the time, and from then until his death sixty-five years later, his literary output of reviews, poems, novels, and plays was prodigious. His first book, *Salt-Water Ballads*, appeared in 1902, and its first edition of five hundred copies sold out in six months. Among the poems in the collection was "Sea Fever," which remains today one of the writer's best-known pieces.

Masefield dedicated the *Ballads* to three women. One of them, Constance Crommelin, an Anglo-Irish schoolteacher, soon became his wife. They had met in 1902, and despite the fact that she was eleven years Masefield's senior, they were married the following year. Their union caused Isabel Fry, the woman with whom Constance had been living for several years, a great deal of anguish, but the two remained close, and the Masefields' first child, born in 1904, was named Isabel Judith, after her mother's friend.

During the next six years, Masefield brought out another book of poetry, three plays, four novels, and six volumes of prose. Late in 1909, when Constance was pregnant again, he became infatuated with another older woman, Elizabeth Robins. She was an American actress and author, nearing fifty—old enough to be Masefield's mother. Indeed after Masefield disclosed that he had lost his mother at an early age the two began addressing one another as "mother" and "son." Robins led him to believe that she too had lost a young son.[11] On his side, the infatuation was intense; he wrote her twice daily. On one occasion, he sent her nine letters during a single day. In this confessional correspondence, Masefield recounted the story of his early life with a frankness and an emotion that are completely lacking in his public commentary. Within a few months, Robins tired of the young poet and broke off the relationship. For the second time in his life, Masefield was suddenly abandoned by a mother. His last letters to Elizabeth Robins are cold and formal; he had been very badly hurt.

The birth of Masefield's son Lewis in July 1910 could not compensate for his loss. In his fifth novel, *The Street of Today* (1911), the hero's sexual frustration and unhappy marriage seem to mirror the author's own. During his life, this novel rarely appeared on lists of Masefield's fiction. In later years, when his marriage and his life were again stable, the work may have embarrassed him.

Masefield's intense involvement with Elizabeth Robins probably helped generate *The Everlasting Mercy*, a highly emotional narrative poem written the following year. The work tells of the transformation of a ne'er-do-well into a God-fearing man, and it brought Masefield both fame and notoriety. Three more long narratives quickly followed. *The Widow in the Bye Street* came out in 1912, and *Dauber* and *The Daffodil Fields* the next year. All sold very well and generated praise, prizes, and parody: John Masefield had become a celebrity.

When World War I broke out, Masefield was thirty-six— too old for the army. Nevertheless, in 1915 he undertook work for the Red Cross in French hospitals. He found it difficult to compose poetry during this period, explaining to Constance, "I could not write, thinking of what goes on in those long slow filthy trains, full of mad-eyed whimpering men."[12] Indeed, Masefield's most affecting writing on the war is to be found in his letters from the front, which have recently been collected.[13] He also traveled to Gallipoli, arriving in the aftermath of the British defeat. In 1916 he patriotically chronicled the battle, likening it to Roland's downfall at Roncevaux at the hands of the Saracens in the ninth century. This romantic interpretation of the disheartening and costly defeat was gratefully devoured by English readers.

Masefield also made a trip to America in 1916. He was to lecture on literature and, at the same time, sample American opinion of the war in Europe for the British government's Propaganda Office. While in New York, he met Florence Lamont, then forty-four and married to a prominent banker. Flattered by her interest in him and disarmed by her intelligence and charm, he may have briefly been in love with her. His first letters to her contain many adoring compliments. The relationship deepened into a lasting friendship, and members of the two families corresponded and visited one another for the next thirty-six years.

When the war ended, Masefield returned to poetry and wrote another well-received narrative poem, *Reynard the Fox* (1919). In the decade that followed, he became increasingly interested in drama. He wrote more plays and produced others at a small theater known as the Music Room built adjacent to his house in Oxford. Financial support for this venture came from the Lamonts. A related interest of Masefield's, the oral recitation of poetry, gave rise to the annual verse-speaking contests at Oxford. He was the guiding spirit behind these events for six years.

When Robert Bridges, England's poet laureate, died in 1930, Prime Minister Ramsay MacDonald had a large pool of talent from which to choose a successor. Yeats, A. E. Housman, Walter de la Mare, Alfred Noyes, and even seventy-five-year-old Rudyard Kipling all would have made distinguished laureates. MacDonald picked Masefield. His choice may have been influenced by Masefield's preoccupation with the working man and by his lack of formal education, for MacDonald was England's first Labor Prime Minister. The selection was well received, and Masefield accepted his job with modesty and enthusiasm, settling easily into the role of wise and dutiful sage. His output continued unabated, but the feeling, the roughness, and the intensity that made his early work so appealing were often buried. Masefield became a public man, instigating awards for young poets, providing platforms for the talented in verse recitation, and generally encouraging literary activity.

His private self escaped into his letters. Interestingly, these personal letters were almost all to women.[14] The fruits of one such friendship have recently been published, Masefield's *Letters to Reyna* (1983). Reyna was Masefield's nickname for Audrey Napier-Smith, a young musician who had written him in 1953 after having heard a radio broadcast of his play *Melloney Holtspur*. Although Masefield met her only five times during his life, his letters to Reyna are warm and affectionate, and full of information about literature and history. Their correspondence continued for fourteen years, up until the poet's death. Writing her was a great source of satisfaction to him, for he was quite alone. He had outlived his wife (who died in 1960 at the age of ninety-three), his son (killed in World War II), and his dear friend Florence Lamont. Only Judith remained with him. In 1967 he contracted gangrene from an infected toenail and refused to have his leg amputated to prolong his life. With Judith at his bedside, he died on May 12, just a few weeks before his eighty-ninth birthday.

Masefield's autobiographical writings are interesting as much for what they leave out as for what they include. *New Chum* (1944), a memoir of his first term aboard the school ship

Conway is by far his most candid. Though written fifty years after the events it narrates, it possesses a remarkable vividness and attention to detail. With characteristic reticence, Masefield identifies no one by name; even those sailors whom he admires most are referred to only by nicknames.

Masefield's adoration of some of the older boys is touching and bespeaks his need for a loving parent figure. One sailor in particular, identified only as H. B., was held in his highest esteem. He slung his hammock next to Masefield's and was fond of hearing ghost stories before he went to sleep. These the young Masefield knew aplenty, and so won the approval of his admired neighbor. Although theirs could hardly be termed a real friendship, H. B.'s kindness deeply impressed Masefield and helped him through his difficult early weeks on board.

When H. B. received his orders and left the *Conway* for a seagoing vessel, Masefield grieved: "Nothing in my boyhood hurt me so cruelly as the loss of H. B." After following his hero's career for several years, Masefield lost track of him: "I know not what became of him; but I have thought of him every day for more than half a century. Surely I was the luckiest of all new chums to have such a man to sling next to at my first coming aboard."

Masefield badly needed this friendship since he was a sensitive boy and the hazing of new chums was severe. In his later autobiographical writings, he rarely recalls in detail any personal feelings of dismay or disappointment, but *New Chum* brims with such emotions. The abundance of swearing, pushing, tripping, and general bullying that fell onto the head of the new chum is painstakingly chronicled. During Masefield's first few days, one senior boy instructed him to pull in the wrong direction during a maneuver: "I who was hauling hard against the strength of perhaps eighty men, went flying . . . violently banging into the double lines of men, and receiving violent kicks and blows from those I hurt." Back

near his hammock the same day someone suddenly shoved
him and he fell back on the deck to be kicked and punched
again. The torture continued. On his first visit to the Liverpool Baths with the ship's company, Masefield was roughly
dunked and nearly drowned.

The vividness of recall of this and other harsh treatment
after fifty years indicates how intensely Masefield felt the
experience. Although the pain of his hazing is evident, he
states: "I was not homesick; I was not unhappy, only completely lost in a new world." Finally, the adjustment was
made, friendships formed, and pleasure taken in the routine
of the ship. Masefield loved going aloft and being able to
survey the Liverpool harbor. He took up meteorology at the
suggestion of an older hand and found his "first delight in
study." He also developed an admiration for the "high endur-
ance" of British sailors and for their sailing ships. When the
sailing vessel *Wanderer* returned to port with tattered sails
and broken masts after weathering a dreadful storm, Masefield reacted with awe: "I had seen nothing like her in all my
life, and knew, then, that something had happened in a world
not quite ours."

There is a vividness in *New Chum* that is also characteristic of Masefield's best poetry. At one point in the memoir he
worries about his ability to relay the intensity of his experience:
"I find I have not been able to tell the effect which the ship had
made upon me. It was profound; it was translation to another
world utterly unlike anything before known, read of, or imag-
ined. I had been plucked up by the roots and pitched endways,
to strike root or die; now the roots were trying to catch something." Such fears about his inability to convey his experiences
were unjustified; he tells his story very well.

But he does not tell it all. His assessment of his time on
the *Conway* to Elizabeth Robins shows that he omitted some
of the seamier parts of his experience. To her he allowed that
"The tone of the ship was infamous. Theft, bullying, barra-

try, sodomy, and even viler vice were rampant." Furthermore, he confessed, "I'd not been on board more than three days when a great hulking brute tried to make me submit to him, and when I refused, he led me such a hell of a life that I nearly drowned myself. I've seen boys committing sodomy on the ship's decks quite openly. I've seen worse things still."[15] There was no way that the Poet Laureate of England could have included such information in his memoir, nor is there any indication that he wished to. Even in his most intimate letters, such personal confessions are rare.

In the Mill (1941) is more detached and less successful than *New Chum*. Written three years before *New Chum*, it covers a later period in Masefield's life—the two years he spent working in the Smith Carpet Mill. The book begins abruptly and never alludes to the circumstances that brought him to America nor to the reasons why he was without employment. The pain surrounding those years must have still affected Masefield as he wrote, for *In the Mill* is a distant and impersonal memoir.

The dedication of the book reads "To Anty, Billy, Dunk, Ed, Eddie, Jacob, Jimmy, Pat, Perce, Smiddy, and Tommy." These were his friends in the mill, but the alphabetical citation suggests that he was not close to any one of them. The reader is afforded little glimpse of these young men. Whether Masefield shared anything other than a loose camaraderie with them on the job is hard to determine. He records no memorable outings in their company and no penetrating conversations with them. Neither is there a glimpse of the young women he met during this time. He does speak of one "friend" a thousand miles away, who falls into some terrible difficulty. The young Masefield immediately starts to save money to help him and even considers making the trip in order to be with him. But who this person is, where he is, and what his particular difficulty might have been, is never revealed.

The reader senses that Masefield, young as he was, felt intellectually far removed from his fellow workers at the mill. Their preoccupation was boxing; his was books. The reading that he did during his years at the mill is as impressive as it is eclectic. He was at the time younger than a college freshman is today, yet he devoured the works of Malory, Melville, Chaucer, Keats, Shelley, and Swinburne. He read English classic novels, Celtic romances, American short stories, and a number of less-notable volumes, which he unaffectedly admits moved him very deeply. His only mentors were bookstore owners. Toward the end of *In the Mill*, Masefield firmly states, "I have nothing but gratitude towards the mill; it gave me a square deal with ample pay for a good day's work and leisure for which I had longed for years; it gave me a chance to study."

Study, however, was not all that Masefield wanted. Two hoped-for promotions were denied, and the dream of attending medical school in America came to nothing. These disappointments and the bitter New York winters chilled and depressed him. In a moment of candor he admitted, "Often I hated the Mill," but his guard comes up again, and no specific detail is offered.

In the Mill ends, not with Masefield's decision to return to England, but with a brief treatise on factory life and its problems. Masefield offers some suggestions to counteract the monotony of factory work and to close the gap between the worker and the designer of the product. He pays compliment to the spirit of American democracy, which gives hope to the factory worker. His fellows, he says, did not resent making carpets that they themselves could not afford: "They were Americans, certain of two things, first that they were every way as good as those who could afford them; and next, that if they bustled and made good, they themselves would be able to afford them. They were defended first by dignity, then by hope; and these two comforts, long denied to European workers, are by no means small."

Masefield seems to have learned from the factory workers more as a group than as individuals. He sympathized with their difficulties and praised their general good spirits. Discontent would erupt only when the mill closed for several weeks. Only then, he observes, did the workers feel "that something blindly and greatly wrong had come down upon their helpless poverty, and that such wrongs should not be. They did not know how to prevent the wrongs; they were incoherent, thoughtless, unpractical; but they were sufferers, have no doubt of that, and in their dumb way, cried for justice."

Did Masefield actually entertain these wise adult thoughts while he was in Yonkers? Most likely not; he was too insecure and unhappy at the time to think much about the misfortunes of others. The passionate tract that comprises the last forty pages of *In the Mill* is the wisdom of a middle-aged Poet Laureate. It is far removed from the main character of the memoir—a solitary, often sickly seventeen-year-old, disgraced and alone in a foreign country.

So Long to Learn, written in 1952, keeps its distance from the pain of actual events, too. It recounts the growth of the poet's literary interests and talents, dwelling on, as he says, "all that has seemed important to me in my effort to become a writer and a teller of tales." Masefield was seventy-four when he wrote this book and in a mood for summarizing and shaping. Certain disappointments, such as his failures as a dramatist, are glossed over philosophically. What emerges is the picture of a person who loved to read, write, and tell stories. These preoccupations were his joy, as well as his solace in times of unhappiness. After his mother's death, the move to his grandfather's house was made bearable because of the wonderful library to be found there.

Masefield mentions, but does not dwell upon, the early

criticisms he received in his struggle to become a writer. Of his aunt's disapproval, he says diplomatically, "It was thought I was too much given to reading." Criticism from the less educated obviously stung less. His inclusion of a *Conway* seaman's comment is calculated to make the reader smile: "What? You a writer? How can you be a writer? Only clever people are writers: and terrible lives they lead both in this world and the next." The ship, however, was part of Masefield's literary education. He admired the sailors' storytelling abilities and tried hard to emulate them.

Masefield's return to England from America marked the turning point in his literary career; harsh criticism gave way to encouragement and praise. His acquaintance with Yeats was pivotal, and his portrait of the Irish poet in *So Long to Learn* is admiring and vivid. Yeats's early poetry and his interest in Irish folklore struck a responsive chord in Masefield, who regretted the English people's inability to mine the folktales from their past.

Toward the end of *So Long to Learn*, Masefield recounts his part in the starting up of the verse recitation contests, and he speaks of his desire to revive the oral tradition in England. The book's peroration, not unsurprisingly, calls for new epics and sagas to further excite the spirit of the English people. The ideas are interesting, but tame; the reader longs for an outburst, but none is forthcoming.

Masefield's last memoir, *Grace Before Plowing*, was published when he was eighty-eight. The elderly poet, steeped as he had been for so many years in his official role as Laureate, predictably speaks only in benign terms. The memories of the landscape of his early childhood are charming, but they give one Herefordshire without Masefield. He observes, but his own presence is hardly felt, and many of the episodes overlap those recounted in *So Long to Learn*. Nevertheless, there is one striking statement the poet makes in this last work. It concerns his parents' attitude towards his reading: "I see now that in those early days my longing for poetry was recognized, and not only permitted, but thoroughly fostered and encouraged. . . . No word was said to me, but the fostering and encouragement were there." This is probably more Masefield's imagination than reality. What is important is that he wished it to be true. All through his long life, Masefield had revised and edited his own story. A year before his death, he was still perfecting his autobiography.

In his early poem "Biography," Masefield predicts that people will not properly understand his life once he is gone:

> When I am buried, all my thoughts and acts
> Will be reduced to lists of dates and facts,
> And long before this wandering flesh is rotten,
> The dates which made me will be all forgotten.

He was only thirty-three when he wrote these lines, but already he was worried about losing control over the copy printed about him. Perhaps the public does not understand the dates that "made" Masefield as well as it might have. Readers certainly know a lot more about him than he ever wished. What would surprise him today is that the public prefers the human being to the saint. Because of our partial intrusion into his privacy, John Masefield is revealed as much more accessible and appealing.

2

••

The Early Lyrics

The *Salt-Water Ballads* (1902) gained Masefield a modest literary reputation. Although the book was ignored by the *London Times*, the public liked the poems and quickly bought up the first edition. As poetry, The *Ballads* seemed to have little in common with late Victorian work, which was often introspective and preoccupied with nature. Tennyson and Swinburne had probed their feelings and reflected on the beauties of the world around them in a lush and sensuous language, but Masefield spoke simply and abruptly. Shying away from his own emotions, he wrote mostly about other people. The *Ballads* grew out of Masefield's experience at sea and his sympathy for his fellow man. The same urge that pushed him toward medical school made him the chronicler of the common sailor: if he could not cure the illnesses of these simple people, at least he could speak understandingly about their lives.

This subject matter also provided a shield for Masefield to hide behind, for in 1902 he did not want to sing of himself or of his experiences. Ironically, the *Ballads* piqued the curiosity of the reading public. They wondered who this sailor-poet was and how he had come to know so much about the sea. Masefield recoiled at their fascination, perceiving that his readers expected a rugged and heroic sailor — something he plainly was not. A letter to his publisher Grant Richards in 1908 reflects his dismay with the public's curiosity: "May I ask you before my novel comes out, to do something for me. I want you not to mention my unhappy past in America and elsewhere to people connected with the press. Those squalid [times? — word illegible] and my early work based upon them have given me a picaresque reputation which is in the way of the serious reputation I now seek."[1]

He had not always found the *Salt-Water Ballads* so embarrassing. Shortly after completing them, he confided to his brother, "I think the book deserves the recognition of a maritime people. It is something new said newly. . . . I feel sure that, in any case, I've said a straight word sure to be recognised as such by some few in the Lord's good time."[2] His mood soon altered, and when Richards wanted to reissue the volume in 1906, Masefield responded: "Don't you think the beastly things are fairly and honestly dead? They would want trimming a good deal, and some would have to come out altogether. I hate every word in the whole book; but I would, I confess, like to purge away some of its faults. However, I think it would be best to let the book die its natural death."[3] Richards acceded to Masefield's wishes but never dropped the idea of reprinting the *Ballads*. A year and a half later, Masefield was still reluctant: "I have come to the conclusion that it would be best not to reprint the ballads; they have no quality which I care to acknowledge now; and I prefer that they should perish."[4] Fortunately, they did not perish; two years later they were again in print, and they stayed in print for half a century.

The style of these early poems is fresh and simple. Masefield avoided using iambic pentameter, perhaps because it was the most common meter in English. Instead, he favored choral repetitions and the galloping anapests of the sea chantey. At the same time, he had the good sense to break up some of these rolling rhythms so that the verses did not become childishly singsong. As a result, many of the ballads are difficult to scan, but the number of accented beats in a line remains regular. Only one poem in the collection, "A Ballad of John

Silver," scans perfectly, and it suffers from this regularity. Even in the first four lines, the problem is apparent:

> We were schooner-rigged and rakish, with a long and
>   lissome hull,
> And we flew the pretty colors of the cross-bones and
>   the skull.
> We'd a big black Jolly Roger flapping grimly at the
>   fore,
> And we sailed the Spanish Water in the happy days of
>   yore.

A common and very effective way Masefield avoided the sing-song measure was by clustering monosyllabic stresses together, as in:

> Clean, green, windy billows notching out the sky,

or in:

> The shuffle of the dancers, the old salt's tale.

All the *Salt-Water Ballads* rhyme, usually very simply. Most use couplets or alternating rhymes, and often the last line is a refrain. Masefield was fond of rhyme, and in his later years made many awkward and trite ones. However, in the *Ballads* the rhymes work well, giving a lyric quality to the thoughtful songs and a lighter touch to the crude, hard-edged tales.

The *Salt-Water Ballads* begin with "A Consecration," Masefield's announcement that his poems are dedicated to the common man. It uses a series of contrasts, which move with speed and feeling as Masefield pits the wealthy and the celebrated against the unsung foot soldiers and spear-carriers who are his heroes. Images of physical discomfort undercut those of pompous celebration:

> THEIRS be the music, the color, the glory, the gold;
> Mine be a handful of ashes, a mouthful of mold.

Alliteration also adds to the poem's impact, emphasizing important words, while pushing the verse forward:

> Not the *r*uler for me, but the *r*anker, the tramp of
> the *r*oad,
> The *s*lave with the *s*ack on his *s*houlders pricked on
> with the goad,
> The man *w*ith too *w*eighty a burden, too *w*eary a load.

Alliteration appears often in the *Salt-Water Ballads*, and one senses that Masefield wished to link his heroes to those whose stories are sung in Old English alliterative poems like "The Seafarer."

The sailor heroes of the *Salt-Water Ballads* are not sentimentalized. Masefield records without apology their poor grammar, their harsh practicality, their wild superstition, their quick tempers. "Evening—Regatta Day" begins with an angry sailor pummeling his fellow:

> Your nose is red jelly, your mouth's a toothless wreck,
> And I'm atop of you, banging your head upon the dirty
> deck.

There is no romance here. Masefield exaggerates the physical damage in order to emphasize how totally his sailors live in the physical world. They tend to express themselves through action rather than language, and when they do speak, it is always in concrete terms. Even the simplest abstractions—words like anger and sorrow—have no place in their vocabularies.

Some of the *Ballads* suggest that the harshness of sea life has robbed the sailors of their sympathy altogether. In "Bill" a seaman's death generates no other feeling than mild annoyance. Because Bill has died, the others will have to take on the work that he would have been doing. Meanwhile, his body lies unmourned, just another piece of junk on an already-messy deck. The images of the metallic moon and sea in the last stanza reflect the hard world of both man and nature that Bill has left behind.

Difficult though sea life is, Masefield's sailors are strongly attached to it. The narrator of "Cape Horn Gospel— I" dies and is buried at sea but then comes back to his ship because he misses the life:

> "I'm a-weary of them there mermaids,"
> Says old Bill's ghost to me;
> "It ain't no place for a Christian
> Below there—under sea.
> For it's all blown sand and shipwrecks,
> And old bones eaten bare
> And them cold, fishy females
> With long green weeds for hair.
>
> "And there ain't no dances shuffled,
> And no old yarns is spun,
> And there ain't no stars but starfish,
> And never any moon or sun."

Despite the blunt and ungrammatical expression, there is poetry in this sailor's soul. His imagination, like a true poet's, is rooted in the physical world, and his perceptions are both playful and astute. The contrast of stars to starfish and the substitution of weeds for a woman's hair create wonderfully evocative images.

Sometimes the speaker in the *Ballads* is not an uneducated sailor but a person like Masefield himself through whose perceptions the mysterious powers of the sea come to life. Although the tone of these poems seems cooler and more reserved than those about sailors or spoken by sailors, the method and the message are familiar. Insistent physical description records the harshness of a life of hard physical struggle. "Cardigan Bay," which first appears to be nothing more than a lively look at the sea on a windy day, turns into an eerie contrast between the wild surface of a treacherous bay and the strange calm that lies below:

> Clean, green, windy billows notching out the sky,
> Grey clouds tattered into rags, sea-winds blowing high,
> And the ships under topsails, beating, thrashing by,
>   And the mewing of the herring gulls.
>
> Dancing, flashing green seas shaking white locks,
> Boiling in blind eddies over hidden rocks,
> And the wind in the rigging, the creaking of the blocks,
>   And the straining of the timber hulls.
>
> Delicate, cool sea-weeds, green and amber-brown,
> In beds where shaken sunlight slowly filters down
> On many a drowned seventy-four, many a sunken town,
>   And the whitening of the dead men's skulls.

The peace at the beginning of the third stanza is deceptive. Those lovely beds of seaweed are graves for drowned sailors, and the shaken sunlight settles over them like a pall. The impassivity and the beauty of the scene mask the sea's destructive power. The welter of activity and the sense of struggle in the first two stanzas are captured by the string of present participles. Notching, blowing, beating, thrashing, mewing, dancing, shaking, boiling, creaking, and straining give way abruptly to the stillness in the third stanza. Those hidden rocks buried in the center of the bay have claimed their victims. Exhilarated by the action and numbed by the beauty of the calm, the reader also tends to miss the phrase "hidden rocks" buried at the center of the poem and, like the sailors, is caught unaware by the treachery of "Cardigan Bay."

The powerful attraction the sea exerts on the individual is the subject of "Sea Fever," one of Masefield's most often quoted poems. The repeated imperative "I must down to the seas again" that begins each stanza suggests the pull of a powerful natural force on the speaker. His response seems irrational, as he explains that "the call of the running tide / Is a wild call and a clear call that may not be denied." Compulsively, he heaps additional demands on his initial request for a ship. The lack of subordination in the syntax of these demands—the equating of every item large or small through the use of the conjunction "and"—underlines the irrationality of the speaker's state of mind.

There is little suggestion of beauty in the particulars that attract the poet to the sea in "Sea Fever." The "grey mist" and the "grey dawn" and the "wind like a whetted knife" present a harsh and gloomy picture. The metaphor of the title, the "fever," reinforces the impression that love of the sea is not an aesthetic experience; it is a visceral one. And though the poem ends with the anticipated contentment of "a quiet sleep and a sweet dream when the long trick's over," the reader recalls two of the other *Salt Water Ballads* with "fever" in the title. In "Fever Ship" and "Fever Chills," the sailors suffer from yellow fever and malaria, and die. The images of their suffering from these very-real sea fevers sharply undercut the euphoria of the metaphorical one.

Another dark quality of the sea appears in "Sorrow of Mydath." An exhausted and depressed speaker longs for the oblivion of death by drowning. The repetition of the words "weary" and "desolate" and the large number of monosyllables lend a mood of hopelessness to the poem. Mydath is a surrogate for Masefield in this poem, and Mydath's weariness reflects the extreme fatigue Masefield suffered during his first years as a writer. Though "Sorrow of Mydath" figures among the best of Masefield's lyrics, the poet on several occasions chose not to reprint it in collections of his poetry. Ever one to

repress the unpleasant in his own life, Masefield must have
feared that his readers would see him as desperate and suici-
dal in his early days. The name Mydath apparently suggested
"my death" too blatantly, so the poet excised it in order to
preserve his privacy.[5]

The year after the *Salt-Water Ballads* came out, Masefield published a second volume of poems simply called *Ballads*. It was expanded and reissued as *Ballads and Poems* in
1910. The two volumes together contained only about forty
new poems, a slim output for an eight-year period. Masefield
admitted in a letter to Yeats that married life, fatherhood, and
other commitments made verse writing very difficult. Prose
was apparently less demanding.[6] The weakest of the new poems were the love lyrics. Happiness was then, as always, a
difficult subject for Masefield to write about. The lines of his
love poems, though sincere, often lack originality.

Masefield is at his best in his early poems when he is
writing about something that has upset him. His anger over
the ripping down of a small Devon village's seawall gave rise
to a fine poem called "Hall Sands." In it he describes the
action of the sea eating away at the town, likening the brute
greed of men to that of the hungry sea. "Hall Sands" appeared
only in the 1903 edition of the *Ballads* and is now virtually
unknown. Masefield probably repressed it because he felt
uncomfortable playing the advocate, and thought it ungentle-
manly to reprint the poem once the furor had died down.
"Hall Sands" is more than just a social protest, however; it is a
fine lyric that belongs in anthologies of English poetry. Particularly striking is the use of enjambment that creates a sense of
the fast-eroding power of the sea on the shore. In the poem's
unusual rhyme scheme (*a b a b b*), the extra *b* rhyme suggests
the uneven contest between the sea and the land. Images of
thievery mingle with those of gluttony so that the destruction
of the village appears to be a moral offense—a sin—rather
than a natural disaster:

The moon is bright on Devon sands,
  The pale moon brings the tide,
The cold green water's greedy hands
  Are clutching far and wide
  Where the brown nets are dried.

Oh! snakey are the salt green waves
  That wash the scattered shells;
They come from making sailors' graves
  And tolling sunk ships' bells—
  But now their tossing swells

Are lipping greedy at the stone
  Which props the scattered town.
They cannot leave the rocks alone,
  They mean to sink and drown
  The wretched cabins down.

The beams are creaking, and the walls
  Are cracking, while the sea
Lips landward steadily and galls
  Those huts of brick and tree
  Which men's homes used to be.

Lithe, wicked eddies twist and spin
  Where once they dragged their boats.
The nimble shrimps are nesting in
  The rye-patch—and the throats
  Of sea-snails glut the oats.

It is all falling, slipping swift;
  The thievish tides intend
To crumble down and set adrift,
  To eat away and rend.
  And steal, and make an end.

Soon, when the wind is setting cold
  And sharp from the south-east,

> The great salt water running bold
>   Will give the fish a feast,
>   And the town will have ceased.

> But that its wretched ruins then—
>   Though sunken utterly—
> Will show how the brute greed of men
>   Helps feed the greedy sea.

If Masefield's indignation helped him to write strong poetry, so did his depression. "C.L.M." explores his guilt over what he perceived as his unpaid debt to his mother and to all women. He expresses sorrow that his mother would not even recognize him were she to return from the grave and pass him on the street. In the last two stanzas, Masefield's mother becomes an emblem of all women and the poet an exemplar of all thankless men. References in the poem to the pains of childbearing probably arose out of his discussions with Elizabeth Robins on the subject. He had sent her an early draft of the poem, referring to her in his letter as one of the "poor, poor heroic agonised mothers." He then humbly asked, "What can sons do to repay you for that horror?"[7]

Masefield's poems of 1903 and 1910 move away from the particularity of description and the irregularity of meter that were the hallmark of the *Salt-Water Ballads*. Abstractions like Beauty and Wisdom make an appearance, and several long poems suffer from an overly regular beat. The poet's attraction to exotic externals, however, remains undiminished:

> Clumsy yellow-metal earrings from the Indians of Brazil,
> Uncut emeralds out of Rio, bezoar stones from Guayaquil;
> Silver, in the crude and fashioned, pots of old Arica
>   bronze,
> Jewels from the bones of Incas desecrated by the Dons.

In all his early lyrics, Masefield's appreciation of the sea and sea life remains double-edged. "Cargoes," the best-known poem from these collections, is no exception. Avoiding both the vagueness and the regularity of his weaker verse, Masefield comments on the passing of time through the description of three cargo-laden ships from three different periods of history. The beauty and romance of the past founder against the grimy industrial present in the last stanza.

Masefield tried to make his early poems sharp and impersonal. He wanted to talk about life at sea without dredging up his own bitter experience. This dual attempt at revelation and obfuscation was not wholly successful. Because his early lyrics told more than he wanted them to, Masefield soon altered his style. He emendation of "Sea Fever" reflects the change. The early version of the poem's first line was syntactically and rhythmically difficult, and these difficulties suggested the speaker's ambivalence toward the sea. When Masefield wrote "I must down to the seas again," he seemed to be resisting a powerful force. With the revision to the more melodious "I must go down to the seas again," some of the poem's tension is dissipated. In this version, the sea appears to be more inviting and the speaker more willing to go. Through this simple change, Masefield subtly negates the suggestion that he may not have wanted to go to sea. The new rhythm tells the reader that he fairly galloped to the shore.

In his early poems Masefield tried to distance himself from the sailors, but he was more like them than he would first admit. Too sensitive and well brought up to brawl and swear, he nevertheless shared their fear and anger. Like them, he was not inclined to speak philosophically or to think deeply about his adventures at sea. His preoccupation with externals and his very sharp observation of the physical world reflect a sensitive mind too frightened to probe. As he became more stable, buoyed first by love and then by fame, Masefield dealt more openly with painful emotions. But his own good fortune served to soften and sentimentalize his perception of pain. Ironically, it is in the early ballads that he is most unguarded and exposed. He knew this. The *Salt-Water Ballads* did not embarrass Masefield — as he told his publisher — because they were bad; they embarrassed him because they were revealing.

3

‣‣

The Narratives

When Masefield turned to narrative verse in 1911, the guarded style of the *Ballads* fell away, and his poetry became unself-conscious and vehement. He discovered that he could write about emotions that wrack the human spirit—religious fervor, sexual jealousy, pride—without flinching and without causing readers to raise their eyebrows knowingly. Furthermore, by manipulating the story line, Masefield found that he could weave his past unhappiness into the fabric of tragedy. In his narratives, instead of hiding behind tight-lipped sailors and picturesque descriptions, Masefield hid behind torrents of emotion. His readers were more interested in their own reactions than in his motivation. Writing about human emotions, then, turned out to be the best mask of all for John Masefield.

Because he loved both poetry and stories, Masefield was naturally drawn to narrative verse. His special admiration for Chaucer added to the appeal of the narrative form. There was a profoundly conservative strain in Masefield, and because of his lack of formal education, he looked to the great writers of the past as instructors. Even the *Salt-Water Ballads*, which seemed experimental to readers and critics, drew life from a form that had been around for hundreds of years. The openness of narrative poetry brought out both the best and the worst in Masefield. The form gave him the freedom to develop both character and action at his own pace, but it also gave him the license to fill the background with extraneous detail.

As a narrative poet, Masefield tended toward the excessive. But what his verse lacked in restraint, it made up for in fervor.

The Everlasting Mercy (1911), Masefield's first narrative poem, tells the story of the conversion of Saul Kane from rogue to decent man. Like his prototype, Saul of Tarsus, Saul Kane feels compelled to tell his story and affirm the role of Christ's mercy in his life. His surname, suggesting that he also bears kinship to the biblical Cain, reinforces the theme of his need for grace.

When it appeared, the poem both entranced and disturbed its readers. Said one critic: "It started excitement because upon its publication nobody could positively decide for all whether it was good or not. It was vehement, the language used by some of the persons depicted in it had all the air of being obscene . . . the revivalist fervor of the later pages was to some very moving, and in fact those who prided themselves upon their fastidiousness were compelled to read it the better to ridicule it."[1]

In the preface to the American edition of the poem, Masefield gave a partial explanation of its genesis:

It began to form images in my mind in the morning of a fine day in May, 1911. I had risen very early and had gone out into the morning with a friend. . . . On our way down a lane in the freshness and brightness of the dew we saw coming toward us, up a slope in a field close by us, a plough team of noble horses followed by the advancing breaking wave of red clay thrust aside by the share. The ploughman was like Piers Plowman or Chaucer's ploughman, a staid, elderly, honest and most kindly man whom we had long known and respected. The beauty and nobility of this sight moved me all day long.

This chaste explanation may well be true, but Masefield often hid his true and painful real feelings. The poem, which treats a cataclysmic change in the protagonist's life, is more likely rooted in the exorcism of Masefield's passion for Elizabeth

Robins and his renewed love for his wife and family. Wherever it came from, *The Everlasting Mercy* tapped a deep well of emotion, and few who read it — even today — can remain unmoved.

An already-converted Saul Kane narrates the story. Normally, this point of view would remove the drama from a poem and run a risk of the narrator's sounding too righteous to be affecting. Masefield skillfully avoids this pitfall; Saul speaks of his past with a directness and an openness that cause the reader to enter into the drama, instead of sitting back and judging it. Because his words spill out so compulsively and in such detail, Saul's story seems less a sermon than a confession.

Saul Kane is not simply a wild man who turns to Christ. He has a conscience, even if he has difficulty acting on its promptings. At the very beginning of the poem, we hear him scolding himself:

> "I'll have no luck tonight," thinks I.
> "I'm fighting to defend a lie.
> And this moonshiney evening's fun
> Is worse than aught I've ever done."

He is also thoughtful. Uneducated though he may be, Saul spends time pondering life's mysteries, even before his conversion:

> "If this life's all, the beasts are better."
> And then I thought, "I wish I'd seen
> The many towns this town had been;
> I wish I knew if they'd a got
> A kind of summat we'd a-not,
> If them as built the church so fair
> Were half the chaps folks say they were."

Unschooled, yet thoughtful; a common man, yet a poet; a dweller among the crude, yet one who is able to see the truth—Saul seems a lot like Masefield himself. He is never seen committing a serious crime, and even when he runs drunk and naked through the streets, he appears to be less a devil than a prophet.

The success of *The Everlasting Mercy* comes from its startling momentum. Saul says that he has converted, yet he describes his fighting, his revelry, and his despair so vividly that one does not believe him capable of change. At several points in the poem he feels pangs of conscience, only to sink deeper into the mire of his misdeeds. With each of his failures to reform, it becomes more certain that he is too hard, too crude, and too proud ever to change his ways. It is this tension between what one sees and what one knows to be true that involves the reader in the poem's drama.

Three important conversations help punctuate the narrative. The story opens with Saul engaged first in a bout of boxing and then in a bout of celebratory drinking. Suddenly disgusted by his own behavior, and the behavior of those around him, he takes to the streets, berating the sleeping townspeople. He is brought up short by the town parson, who convincingly answers his wild harangue.

A second debate evolves, uninitiated by Saul, with a woman whose child has been lost in the market. After staying with the boy, feeding him, and telling him stories until his mother appears, Saul finds his recent kindness held inconsequential when weighed against his past sins. The child's mother sees him only as a wastrel who lead her older children astray. She, like the parson, rebuts Saul's arguments and diminishes his stature by contrasting her life of hard work with the carousing and lewdness that mark his own. Her speech impresses him and, unwilling to ponder its implications, he heads back to the pub. There he taunts a Quaker woman whose practice it is to come

> To all the pubs in all the place,
> To bring the drunkards' souls to grace;
> Some sulked, of course, but some were stirred,
> But none give her a dirty word.

By overstepping the boundary and giving the woman a "dirty word," Saul elicits a stirring plea from her. She speaks not of society, as the parson did, nor of the individuals Saul has harmed, as the mother did; she speaks instead of Christ. The urgent quality of the message and the personal involvement of the speaker move Saul to accept the Christ who, he realizes, has always accepted him. He walks out into the dawning day and meets the honest plowman. Stepping behind the plow, he begins to work—a new man.

The deliberateness of the debate in *The Everlasting Mercy* gives needed weight to the almost-breathless verse. Masefield's iambic tetrameter and numerous feminine end rhymes cause the poetry practically to rattle as it speeds along. Frequent use of a series of four verbs or four adjectives also conveys a sense of the action piling up and rolling along. These stylistic qualities and the strong emotional tone of the poem make it easy to parody. Yet those who began poking fun at it ended up discovering its intense power. Said poet Siegfried Sassoon:

After the first fifty lines or so, I dropped the pretense that I was improvising an exuberant skit. While continuing to burlesque Masefield for all I was worth, I was really feeling what I wrote—and doing it not only with abundant delight, but a sense of descriptive energy quite unlike anything I had experienced before.[2]

A second long narrative, *The Widow in the Bye Street* (1912), quickly followed *The Everlasting Mercy*. Though well received, it was considered by many as inferior to its predecessor. Written in seven-line stanzas of rhyme royal, it lacks the drive of the earlier poem. The intricate requirements of its rhyme scheme tax Masefield's abilities, and there seem to be many forced lines. Structurally, the poem is divided into six parts, but it has neither the dynamic punctuation of incidents that make up Saul Kane's story, not its engaging first-person narrator. Both the rhyme scheme and the subject matter suggest that Masefield was looking to Chaucer's *Troilus and Criseyde* for inspiration.

In the narrative, the innocent young Jim Guerney becomes infatuated with a beautiful and flirtatious young widow named Anna. Jim's hardworking and overprotective mother, also a widow, completes the triangle. The gulf between the two widows yawns wide, and the distance between youth and age, sensuality and wisdom, careless interest and dogged devotion proves impossible for Jim to bridge. Thrown over by Anna upon the return of one of her former lovers, he becomes maddened with jealousy. He attacks his rival with a plowshare, accidentally killing him, and is quickly jailed, tried, and hanged.

The beautiful Anna sheds a few tears and starts out again in a new town where she quickly forgets her grief. Sensual even with nature's creatures, she can steal the birds' attention away from the virginal roses:

> One heard her in the morning singing sweet,
> Calling the birds from the unbudded rose,
> Offering her lips with grains for them to eat.

The old widow finds another kind of satisfaction—in madness. The poem's last scene shows her, a pathetic parody of her rival, singing crazily and putting flowers in her hair.

The Widow in the Bye Street provides an interesting insight into Masefield's life in 1912. At the height of his passion for Elizabeth Robins, Masefield had promised her in a letter that "all my work from this [time] on shall be done for the cause of women."[3] A year and a half later he mocked his noble feelings in the creation of the faithless Anna. Physically, Anna resembles Robins, with her brilliant blue eyes and manipulative ways. The divided loyalty Jim feels toward the two older women mirrors Masefield's relationship with Robins and his wife. Like Jim, Masefield was naively flattered by an older woman's intimacy with him, unaware that she had been close to other men and incredulous that she could so quickly drop him. In the end, however, Masefield could not bring himself to destroy Anna fully. Selfish and faithless as she is, she remains more appealing than the good mother, and she is without doubt the most interesting character in *The Widow in the Bye Street*.

Masefield delved into another area of his personal life with *Dauber* (1913). This narrative tells the tragic tale of a sensitive young seaman who aspires to be an artist. Just like Masefield, Dauber finds himself on a ship that becomes locked in ice for a month around Cape Horn. Physically and temperamentally he also resembles the author, "a slight-built man, / Young for his years . . . bullied and damned at since the voyage began." In *Dauber*, however, Masefield romanticizes his own experience by having the young man gain acceptance as a sailor during the ordeal around the Cape. When in a final storm he falls to his death from aloft, he is mourned by the hard seamen who had once mocked him.

From one perspective, *Dauber* is less a mirror of Masefield's time at sea than it is a mask. The most important details of the story have been changed. Masefield ended his voyage a Distressed British Seaman; Dauber ends his a hero. Perhaps Masefield revealed this portion of his past precisely so that he might transform it and exorcize its ugly memory.

Although written in the same verse form as *The Widow in the Bye Street*, *Dauber* unfolds much more easily. Masefield is now willing to break the regularity of an iambic pentameter beat, and he loosens his allegiance to the end-stopped line. Often the narrative spills from one line to the next and even from one stanza to the next. Masefield does not stop the flow of an incident—for example, the Dauber's fall—just because a stanza comes to an end. In fact, by letting the action spill over from the place where the pause is expected, he is able to convey the speed of the descent.

Masefield neither moralizes the Dauber's tale nor frames it with foreboding. As a result, it seems more immediate than either of his two previous narratives. The reader sympathizes with the Dauber's discomfort and loneliness, and is as bewildered as the young man himself when he falls to his death. As a character, the Dauber is more fully realized than either Saul Kane or Jim Guerney. Through flashbacks, the reader learns of the young man's difficulties with his farmer father and of his closeness to his mother who painted in secret in order to escape her husband's derision. Incidents on shipboard further illustrate the Dauber's reticence and his pluck. He seems foolish and rigid when, after hours aloft in the ice storm, he refuses whiskey because he has taken an oath of temperance. But this same stubbornness enables him to continue drawing, despite the taunts of the unlettered sailors.

Masefield is often guilty of overloading the background of his narratives, but in *Dauber* the descriptions deepen the texture of the story. The metaphors evoke the discomfort and constraint of manning a ship during a violent storm:

> A moment now was everlasting hell,
> Nature an onslaught from the weather side,
> A withering rush of death, a frost that cried,
> Shrieked, till he withered at the heart; a hail
> Plastered his oilskins with icy mail.

Images of nature as an aggressive adversary and the ship as a besieged town reinforce the notion of life at sea as uneven combat. Like a young knight in his "icy mail," Dauber is tested both physically and spiritually in the combat:

> In the great tempest's fiercest hour, began
> Probation to the Dauber's soul, of pain
> Which crowds a century's torment into a span.
> For the next month the ocean taught this man,
> And he, in that month's torment, while she wested
> Was never warm, nor dry, nor full, nor rested.

The year *Dauber* appeared also saw the publication of a slightly longer narrative, *The Daffodil Fields*. Generally considered inferior to the three earlier narratives, the poem remains interesting because of Masefield's evenhanded treatment of the three central characters who are caught up in a love triangle. The steady and sober Lion Occleve loves Mary Weir and behaves throughout most of the story with a restraint and civility that belie his name. Mary appreciates these virtues but, like many of her sex, she loves instead the careless, handsome Michael Grey. Michael possesses many of the qualities associated with the villains of Masefield's early novels, and one expects the poet to side with Lion who, with his patient devotion and gentlemanly acquiescence, resembles Masefield himself. Even his name suggests that he will be king in the end. Not so, and herein lies the surprise and the strength of the poem. Michael falls in love with Mary and goes to South America to earn money so that they may wed. The wild plains of Argentina suit him so well, however, that he soon forgets promises made in England. Although from an ethical standpoint Michael is behaving very badly, Masefield shows sympathy for him and is careful not to make him seem rakish, vile, or consciously cruel.

After discovering that Michael is living with another woman in Argentina and has no intention of returning home, Mary enters into a loveless marriage with Lion. The reader's expectation that she will gradually warm to her virtuous husband is never fulfilled. Instead, Masefield has Mary contrive to bring Michael back by sending him a wedding announcement and an old love token. The communication has the desired effect, and Michael returns to England, conscious of his past errors. Masefield does not fault Mary for her actions, even when she leaves her husband to live with Michael. He does not even comment on her behavior, and through this omission suggests that Mary only dimly understands what she is doing. Duty and convention mean nothing to her in the end. They mean even less to Lion when he is finally roused. Inevitably, the poem ends with all three characters dead, victims of passions they could not control.

Masefield frames each of the six sections of the poem with a reference to the daffodil fields where Lion, Michael, and Mary used to play as children. Initially, the flowers present an amoral backdrop against which human passions unfold. The reader understands that nature follows its own cycle of death and rebirth, unaffected by the pageant of human emotion. But by the end of the poem, the characters themselves become identified with the flowers, and the reader sees them, like the daffodils, responding to irrational inner promptings rather than the rule of reason.

A prose synopsis of *The Daffodil Fields* makes it sound more compelling than it actually is. Much of the poetry is pedestrian and the story is too drawn out. Part of the difficulty stems from Masefield's decision to vary his rhyme royal stanzas by making the last line an alexandrine. This final hexameter line forces the poet to pause at the end of each stanza, and gives the story a halting quality.

When World War I broke out, Masefield abruptly stopped writing narratives and turned to more-contemplative forms of poetry. The sustained effort necessary to generate a long narrative was probably impossible during the war years. With the 1918 armistice came a complicated flood of emotions. Weary of tragedy and brimming with patriotic feeling, Masefield produced an entirely new kind of narrative — *Reynard the Fox* (1919). The poem provides an almost-escapist picture of England at play. One meets in it a startling array of characters from every social class, gathered together to participate in a day of fox hunting. The story unfolds in easy iambic pentameter couplets, allowing Masefield to concentrate more on his story and less on his rhyme schemes.

Reynard was greatly appreciated by a war-weary nation and touted by several critics as Masefield's masterpiece. Although it contains many stirring moments, it is entirely too long, as even its greatest admirers will admit. The introduction of the hunt's participants and spectators takes up fully one-third of the poem. This catalogue of characters contains some fine poetry, but the reader finds it disconcerting to meet so many people who appear only to drop immediately out of the narrative. In fact, not one of these people plays a significant role in the poem; the fox is the only important character.

The first section of *Reynard* is Masefield's homage to the prologue of Chaucer's *Canterbury Tales*, and it suffers by the inevitable comparison. Not only is Chaucer's narrative verse more lively, his overall structure is more elaborate and better proportioned. His Canterbury pilgrims are introduced so that the reader may appreciate the kinds of stories they tell and their interaction with one another. Chaucer's prologue of eight hundred lines represents only a small fraction of a long collection of tales. Masefield had no such grand design, and his large cast of characters appears disproportionate in *Reynard the Fox*.

The poet's sharp eye for physical and psychological detail in *Reynard* has been justly praised, but after meeting a number of interesting characters, the reader feels cheated that they do not figure in the remainder of the poem. The chase is related from the point of view of the fox and, like the catalogue, it goes on too long. With the exception of the three occasions when Reynard comes upon burrows that have been stopped up, the tale of the hunt is strangely undramatic. Only at the very end does the action fully engage the reader.

Reynard survives because the hunters pick up the trail of a second fox that they are able to trap and kill. Thus Masefield is able to have it both ways: his sportsmen are satisfied, and the heroic fox is able to retain his freedom. Having suffered through World War I, where even the winners lost heavily, Masefield found relief in telling a tale where everyone wins. However, the death of the second fox and the misguided satisfaction of the hunters leave the thoughtful reader uneasy. Can both sides ever win the same contest?

When one delves into the nature of the fox himself, one finds that he is not really animal-like at all. During the course of the hunt, he is shown to be capable not only of understanding but also of thinking and even wishing. Indeed Reynard resembles no one so much as the hunted heroes Hi Ridden and Sard Harker who appear in Masefield's postwar fiction.

Right Royal (1920) is usually discussed as if it were a rewriting of *Reynard the Fox* with a steeplechase replacing the fox hunt and the horse Right Royal playing the role of Reynard. Considered as a whole, *Right Royal* surpasses *Reynard* as a piece of narrative. Better paced and more dramatic, the story itself is more unified. Two protagonists, the horse Right Royal and his owner, Charles Cothill, share the action. The race itself becomes more than just sport when Charles foolishly bets his entire fortune on Right Royal after having received a message in a dream. Interestingly, Masefield does not condemn Charles for his action or deny the value of a message from the spiritual world. Charles regrets the excessiveness of the bet, but he never doubts the validity of the dream. Consequently, the race takes on a metaphysical cast. Charles and Right Royal are not only racing for a fortune; they are racing for an idea.

Masefield stresses the teamwork of horse and rider, and how each compensates for the other's shortcomings. Through no fault of his own, Charles falls early in the race and seems a beaten man, but he presses on. His progress from last to first place keeps the narrative lively, but the quality of the poetry is not the best. The rolling anapests, chosen by Masefield to imitate the cadence of the galloping horses' hooves, quickly become tiresome.

Right Royal should not be looked at as a patriotic or nostalgic poem in the manner of *Reynard the Fox*. Masefield formulated it as a dual contest of man against man, and man against fate. He conceived the poem as a minor epic and made free use of such devices as the Homeric simile and the epic catalogue. The catalogue of the horses is well done, but most of the similes are dry and flat. In the end, *Right Royal* comes across as a good story but a weak poem. It marks the end of Masefield's widely read narratives. From time to time he attempted others, but they lacked immediacy. Both the poet and the public had lost interest in narrative verse.

Masefield's six famous narratives are the product of a single decade. When he began them, he was a scarcely known writer, torn by feelings of insecurity and rejection. The first three poems acted as a kind of therapy for him, providing an outlet for his pent-up feelings of love and shame. As he gained understanding and became more tolerant and fatalistic about the human condition, Masefield wrote with less force. After the war, his work took on a new quality, becoming more public and more "professionally" English. Ten years before he was named Poet Laureate, Masefield had already begun to see himself as a spokesman for the nation. He liked the role and was happy to trade nagging personal despair for the serenity that fame and patriotism brought him.

4

The Novels

Masefield's fiction is for the most part unknown or ignored, yet it mirrors his career and his interests, often providing considerable insight into his character. As such, it forms an important supplement to his biography. In all, Masefield wrote twenty-one novels. They are by no means consistent in subject matter or quality. Some are readable and compelling, but more than a few are tedious and awkward.

It is intriguing to speculate why Masefield continued to write novels after he was acclaimed as a poet. In the early years, before his reputation was established, he seemed to be looking for the most appropriate medium for his talent and therefore tried his hand at poems, plays, and novels. As his fame as a poet increased, however, his output of fiction continued unabated. Except for a hiatus during World War I and its aftermath, Masefield produced novels almost yearly between 1908 and 1941.

There is no clear-cut reason why this should be. Certainly his interest in writing for children kept him generating novels. Five of his works of fiction—*Jim Davis, Martin Hyde, Lost Endeavour, The Midnight Folk*, and *The Box of Delights*—were aimed at young people who were not yet ready to tackle the rigors of poetry. Masefield thought he had something to communicate to children about the thrill of adventure and also about the tamer virtues fostered in a stable and loving home. One reviewer complained that it was absurd for children's authors to assume that all adventuresome boys end up wanting to go home.[1] Masefield knew better. As a young boy who experienced more than his share of excitement, he never stopped longing for the loving home he did not have.

Another explanation why Masefield never abandoned the novel is simply that he loved stories. Over and over in his writings he speaks of his early fascination with tales of adventure. Sea stories, ghost stories, tales of cowboys and Indians—their hold on him never loosened. And he assumed, quite rightly, that many adults felt the same way. Many of his novels are therefore nothing more than good stories for adults who, like himself, loved fast-paced adventure. He refused to look down on these people as children who were not ready for poetry. To Masefield, every great writer was first of all a good storyteller.

The most important reason why Masefield continued to write so much fiction is one that he himself did not wholly appreciate. He was a self-educated man who never had the opportunity to go to the university. His phenomenal output reflects his insecurity in the world of letters. It is as if he were compensating for his lack of formal education with his amazing productivity. Such a show of diligence can be seen as a form of homage to literature. Because Masefield's novelistic output is so uneven, those who have had the benefits of higher education shake their heads and wish he had written less and been more discerning in what he did write. But this attitude reveals the very qualities that Masefield lacked. His mind never became exclusive and critical; it was always inclusive and accepting.

Was he also hungry for fame? Did he desire to be known as a literary giant—Chaucer and Dickens and Shakespeare rolled into one? Probably not, but he wanted to be recognized as a serious writer, and he therefore compulsively attacked every genre to insure himself some fame in at least one area.

The early novels grope in several different directions with varying success. *Captain Margaret* (1908), Masefield's first published work of fiction (he wrote several others that he destroyed), is among his best. The *Times Literary Supplement* commented that the author had "veiled his whole story — full-blooded and violent as it is — in an alluring and quite appropriate melancholy."[2] Set in the late seventeenth century, the book tells the story of Captain Charles Margaret, a sensitive man thwarted in love. He sets out in his ship, appropriately named *The Broken Heart*, to wrest some trading outposts in Central America from the hands of the Spanish. Fate brings Olivia Stukeley, the young lady who has spurned him, on board *The Broken Heart* with her handsome but worthless husband, Tom. He has married her for her money, and his consuming greed leads him to commit forgery as well. To this, and to his many boorish traits, Olivia remains blind. Margaret gallantly suffers, never seeking to disabuse Olivia of her misconceptions. He incurs gunshot wounds, personal abuse, and the opprobrium of the state, all in an effort to spare her feelings. The book is unabashedly romantic, with the gallant Margaret triumphing in the end over the lusty cad Stukeley.

Masefield admitted to having based his pitiless portrait of Stukeley on someone he had known at the Yonkers Carpet Factory.[3] Says the narrator of him, "By accident of birth, he was a gentleman, [but he was] designed by nature for the position of publican." Masefield had met many such men and recoiled from the way they used their pedigrees as a license to dominate both women and men. He paints Stukeley as a man without finesse or wit. In contrast, Margaret (as his name suggests) possesses many of the so-called feminine qualities that make a person civilized. He is considerate, observant, and responsive to art and beauty — a poet as well as a sea captain. Like Masefield, he has an appreciation of women's feelings: "He had learned much of women. He understood them emotionally with a clearness which sometimes frightened him." Olivia finally sees her error and pledges her love to Captain Margaret. Her disillusionment with Tom parallels

Margaret's with his idealistic commercial scheme. He had innocently thought that his army of privateers might peacefully take over the Spanish-American town of Tolu. Instead, his men rape, pillage, and burn. Margaret's failure helps put Olivia's foolish love for Tom into perspective.

Multitude and Solitude (1909) and *The Street of Today* (1911), together with the much-later *Eggs and Baker* (1936), comprise what might be termed Masefield's social novels. In these stories the hero is unhappy with society as he sees it, and he finds his own ideals in conflict with those of the people around him. Satisfaction comes to him in the end not from changing the society but from self-knowledge and the acceptance of his own limitations.

All three books are riddled with narrative problems, but *Multitude and Solitude* borders on the unreadable. Masefield voiced his sense of its weakness to his publisher: "I've only done about 15,000 words of *Multitude and Solitude*; and what I have done is a sad mess, all bad psychology + colorless prose + there isn't time to get it typed + it is so bad, I hardly like to let you take it as it stands."[4] It is indeed a "sad mess," an undramatic and awkwardly-put-together tale of one Roger Naldrett, a young playwright whose professional and personal lives have reached an impasse in London. Seeking new experience, Naldrett takes the unlikely step of going to Africa to observe and perhaps cure sleeping sickness. His companion, Lionel Heseltine, has been in the field before working on the disease, but like Naldrett, he has limited medical training. After a series of misadventures, the two contract the sleeping sickness themselves but are saved by an original medication that Roger fortuitously concocts and administers.

Bad as it is, *Multitude and Solitude* provides two useful insights into Masefield's life in 1909. First, the reader can appreciate his acute insecurity and worry that the artist's life he had chosen was both self-indulgent and impractical. In

Multitude and Solitude Masefield is still wrestling with the notion that he should have gone to medical school. At one point Roger muses, "What if poetry were a mere antique survival which attracted the fine mind and held it in dalliance?" Such was Masefield's worry as well.

The relationship between Roger's fiancée Ottalie Fawcett and her friend Agatha provides another insight into Masefield's state of mind in 1909. The friendship between the two women mirrors the one between Masefield's wife Constance and Isabel Fry. In *Multitude and Solitude* Agatha, because of her jealousy of Roger, fails to deliver a letter from him that would have delayed Ottalie in London and saved her from being drowned in a ferry accident. Admitting her selfishness to Roger afterward, Agatha confesses, "I was jealous of you. I did all I could to keep you apart. She was in love with you." Masefield's resentment of Isabel's claim on Constance's affections must have run very deep indeed in order to generate so thinly disguised a rebuke.

If *Multitude and Solitude* affords a glimpse into Masefield's personal life, *The Street of Today* provides a great deal more. "Good Lord," he exclaimed to Elizabeth Robins in a letter, "I've hidden a lot of my secret life in my books."[5] *The Street* tells the story of Lionel Heseltine, freshly back from Africa, and Rhoda Derrick, the beautiful but empty young woman whom he marries. Although the first part of the narrative is marked by choppiness and wooden dialogue, the story unexpectedly comes to life when Lionel and Rhoda's marriage begins to founder. Lionel finds his wife both sexually unresponsive and jealous of his work on a fledgling weekly newspaper. The vigor of their fights and the detail and understanding that goes into the description of their feelings make the novel both realistic and dramatic.

Several of Masefield's preoccupations emerge in *The Street of Today*. His disgust with the idle members of upper-class British society is clear, but he also dramatizes the terrible physical toll that a life of hard work can exact. He is drawing on his own experience with overwork as he writes about Lionel's:

It seemed to stretch on and on, as work does. He was always lavish of himself when there was work to do. He did not spare himself. London, never kind to workers, added to his worries by wracking his nerves. His eyes were heavy in his head. His face began to wear the hopeless look of the overworked.

He was away from half past eight till seven, every day. He came home tired out, sat with Rhoda for a time, then buckled to work again. Often he wrote far into the night, trying to get things done. Rhoda felt that she was neglected. She was petulant and peevish. . . . He was very tired. He spoke confusedly, from a brain too weary to be nicely tactful. There was an edge on his speech that should have warned her.

Although Masefield sympathizes with Lionel's dilemma, he also demonstrates considerable understanding of Rhoda's social and sexual behavior as she complains,

Ever since I married you, I've loathed myself. I'm not your wife. Your work is your wife. Your work. A rag which I wouldn't have in the house. I am the housekeeper who is to degrade herself to you in your spare moments so that you might have children. Children. . . . Do you know what children mean to me? If I thought I were going to have a child, I would kill myself. My mother had children. She had nine children in eleven years. They all died except me and Jane. I was the last. I killed her. I got my love of children from my mother. . . . I'm not going through what she went through.

In the end, however, Lionel, and Masefield behind him, find it hard to respect women like Rhoda:

What is she? The beautiful, charming woman, delicate and delightful, accomplished, expensive, all on the surface. Below the surface, nothing. Selfishness perhaps, pretentiousness, tactlessness, want of all nobleness, want of everything except the deadness of the deeply vulgar.

But Masefield is no misogynist. Mary Drummond, the older woman of the novel, has both a social conscience and a personal sensitivity. Like Lionel, she has made an unfortunate marriage and she becomes both his friend and his savior. Based on Elizabeth Robins, Mary is beautiful, independent, and active in the women's suffrage movement. Like Robins, she did not voluntarily choose her lot. Fate leaves her without a responsible husband (he is an alcoholic) and without children. Lionel perceives Mary's sense of loss over not having children and a home, but at the same time he understands that her nobility and her sensitivity stem from the fact that she has not been forced into the traditional woman's role.

Intervening between *Multitude and Solitude* and *The Street of Today* are three adventure novels written for teenage boys.[6] Where the two "serious" novels limped and stumbled, these three rush along. *Martin Hyde* (1909) is a historical novel about a thirteen-year-old boy who falls in with rebels who are trying to put the Duke of Monmouth on the throne of King James II. Filled to the top with unsavory characters, incidents of bold trickery, secret passages, sleeping drafts, and wild chases, the book does not lack for excitement. The young hero, like Masefield at age thirteen, is orphaned and sent to live with an uncle. He is spunky—"a wild disobedient young rogue"—but not without the virtues of sensitivity and loyalty. Every so often Martin even lectures his readers on such topics as the importance of using one's leisure time well or the impossibility of a decent person's committing a murder.

Like *The Street of Today, Martin Hyde* contains an older female character who plays the dual role of friend and savior to the hero. She is Amelia Carew, a loyalist to the king. Despite his own political affiliation, Martin greatly admires

Amelia, and the feeling is reciprocated. At the story's climax, it is she and her uncle who rescue him from a firing squad. Exciting though his life may be, Martin is an easily recognizable variety of the Masefield hero—rough and wild on the surface, but underneath decent and almost prim.

In this book, as in many of his early novels, Masefield shows his remarkable ability to understand and to enter into the imaginative life of other people. Martin Hyde lives out every teenage boy's fantasy. His adventures bring him recognition from influential men and admiration from sexually attractive older women. He has the freedom to do what he likes, unencumbered by family ties, yet in the end he gains the love and security of a new family.

Lost Endeavour (1910), like *Martin Hyde*, takes place in the seventeenth century and has a young teenage narrator. Although it contains many of the same elements of boyhood fantasy, there is a brittle edge to the adventure and more disgust at the seamy side of such a life. At one point, the dejected hero, Charles Harding, says of himself, "I was an innocent boy torn from his home by kidnappers, sold into slavery, and now torn from slavery by pirates." He has no love for the sea. To him sailors are "a hard and vicious company with a few good among them, but not many." And he sees his ship as "a prison, a college where I should learn vice, a temple where I should be consecrated to the gallows." These words echo a letter to Elizabeth Robins in which Masefield recounts the story of his early life and his disgust for the sea after the *Gilcruix* experience. Retelling the story to her seems to have tapped a well of bitterness in the poet that spilled over into the novel. Interestingly, *Lost Endeavour* does not conclude with Charles's return to his family. This open-endedness adds to its disturbing quality.

With *Jim Davis* the following year (1911), the anger disappears, and the reader is again presented with a neat fantasy. The young teenage hero, like Martin Hyde and

Masefield, loses his parents at an early age and comes to live with a reserved aunt and uncle. Of his parents, he says simply and movingly, "It was very sad at home after Mother died; my father shut himself up in his study, never seeing anybody. When my father died, my uncle came to Newham from his home in Devonshire; my old home was sold then and I was taken away." These events certainly draw on Masefield's memories of his own childhood, but the novel is a fantasy and Jim, unlike Masefield, gains a loving surrogate mother, a parson's wife whom he calls Mims. Abandoned by a drunken husband, she moves in with Jim's aunt and uncle and becomes their housekeeper. Soon after, Jim is captured by smugglers. He enjoys many adventures and suffers considerable ill treatment before being reunited with his loved ones.

Jim Davis was written at the same time or perhaps shortly after *The Street of Today*. Though seemingly on another plane, it too reflects Masefield's attachment to Elizabeth Robins. Here again one finds the good mother-woman yoked to a disreputable husband who has abdicated his responsibilities. Mims, like Mary Drummond, ends the book as the strong ally and companion of the young hero. Masefield even goes so far as to have Jim never marry. Instead, he chooses to live out his life with the loving older woman.

Thirteen years intervened between *Jim Davis* and *Sard Harker* (1924). During this period Masefield wrote some of the best poetry of his career, much of it in long narratives. Apparently these narrative poems satisfied Masefield's urge to tell stories for a while, but he could not stay away from the novel indefinitely. *Sard Harker* begins awkwardly as if Masefield has lost his touch, but it turns into a complicated thriller with the hero combing the coast and the mountains of Central America in order to find a kidnapped young woman. He rides freight trains, escapes from jail, falls into the hands of a devil worshipper, is wounded by a stingray and then nearly sucked under by quicksand before he succeeds in his quest.

Wild and unlikely though many of Sard's adventures are, Masefield records them with verisimilitude.

ODTAA (Masefield's coy acronym for "one damn thing after another") (1926) brings more of the same kind of high adventure with the twist that in this novel the young hero, Hi Ridden, fails on his mission. His sufferings and brushes with death are more difficult to accept because neither his personal effort nor the cause for which he is working succeeds. All of Masefield's adventure stories are shot through with realism, but ODTAA is unique in its unhappy ending. Hi Ridden's failure is not tragic; it is disturbingly lifelike.

Masefield veered away from this harsh realism in *The Hawbucks* (1929), the story of an adventuresome young man, George Childrey, who has come from wandering in America to become master of his family estate. Like the rest of the men in the countryside, he falls in love with his beautiful and engaging neighbor, Carrie Herridew. She is the book's most complex character, a young woman both dismayed and delighted by her powers over the opposite sex. At the story's end, her choice for a husband is not George, but his oily and overbearing younger brother Nick, an ambitious and successful lawyer.

Carrie, like many of Masefield's heroines, betrays the author's ambivalence toward the beautiful young women he kept meeting in English society. He could not deny their sexual attractiveness, yet he saw that their upbringing encouraged them to be shallow and hedonistic. Like George, Masefield was drawn physically to women whom he found spiritually unacceptable. Although there are fleeting suggestions in *The Hawbucks* that Carrie is both calculating and without much depth, neither George Childrey nor Masefield can bring himself to say so.

Masefield's inability to separate his sensibility from George's leaves the reader perplexed. The author needs to condemn Carrie for her frivolity and for the calculated choice of a mate whom she clearly does not love. Masefield will not do it. In fact, he abruptly ends the book after Carrie's decision comes to light. This casting away of the novel before it is properly finished is unfortunate because all the elements for a satisfying resolution of the plot are already in place. The book needs to be about fifty pages longer than it is in order for its author to deal with all the loose threads. There is a better woman for George to marry — Carrie's bastard half sister Margaret. George has met her and aided her on several occasions, yet Masefield does not dramatize their final courtship. He simply and lamely announces their inevitable union in the last sentence of the novel.

Why did Masefield so abruptly break off what might have been one of his best novels? *The Hawbucks*, like almost all of his other fiction, is three hundred pages long. Was Masefield unable to sustain himself in a longer work? In 1929, on the eve of being named Poet Laureate, he certainly was not still driven by financial pressures to keep grinding out as much work as possible. More likely, he simply lost interest in *The Hawbucks* and in all his novels when they became "novel length." The chopped-off endings of this and of several of his other novels argue that though Masefield loved stories, he did not love novels. He liked action and adventure, but he cared little for the structural elements necessary to make a novel successful and lasting.

In a three-year period shortly after being named Poet Laureate, Masefield published three sea-adventure novels. *The Bird of Dawning* (1933) tells the exciting story of a ship race, a ship wreck, and a ship takeover. Cruiser Trewesbury, the twenty-two-year-old second mate of the sailing ship *Blackgauntlet*, takes command of the surviving crew after the ship sinks in a storm. He has been abused by the ship's neurotic Captain Duntisbourne and has had other difficulties on previous voyages. His assumption of leadership over the ship-wrecked men therefore becomes a test of his manhood. The book captures well the dangers and discomforts that were daily fare for the crew of a sailing vessel. Masefield is especially effective in showing how the responsibility and the isolation of command can warp the character of a sea captain.

The Taking of the Gry (1934) demonstrates that Masefield is capable of writing a tightly structured novel. This account of the theft of a boat full of munitions during a war between two principalities on the Spanish Main contains enough power and suspense to rival any modern thriller. Not to be confused with a wild sea yarn, *The Taking of the Gry* is accurate and detailed in a totally believable way. The technical difficulties of stealing a boat and then piloting it through an unlighted, fog-bound sea channel are carefully laid out. Because the book has a limited number of characters and a limited length, it stands out as one of Masefield's best works of fiction.

In contrast, *Victorious Troy* (1935) is sprawling and drawn out. It has at its core the interesting plot of a disabled ship that loses half her crew and is piloted into port by the seventeen-year-old apprentice sailor. Unfortunately, Masefield dwells much too long on the action of the killer storm, and he dissipates the suspense with too much attention to the physical damage done to the ship's rigging. His fascination with the mechanics of sailing ships interferes with his story.

Victorious Troy marks the end of Masefield's sea novels. His next four books, written between 1936 and 1939, tell the adventures of three different members of the Mansell family. *Eggs and Baker* (1936), an attempt at a Dickensian novel of character and social commentary, is simply too long. Just as in *Victorious Troy* Masefield spent too much time describing a storm, in *Eggs and Baker* he dwells too long over a trial. The story is an interesting one, but it is not properly paced. Robert Mansell, a good-hearted and none-too-intelligent

baker, becomes a social activist, thereby making himself un-
popular in the small town of Condicott. When the town half-
wit is implicated as an accessory to a murder, Robert springs
to his defense. This stand puts him in the awkward position
of defending the actual murderer as well, for the two have
been charged together. The trial goes badly and the excitable
baker throws eggs at the judge, an action that results in his
own imprisonment and the near ruin of his family. It is obvi-
ous that Masefield cared deeply about the persecution of the
eccentric individual by society, but he was dealing with details
of law and government for which he had little understanding.
As a result, the book is tedious and undramatic.

The Square Peg (1937) introduces Mansell's grandson,
Frampton, a wealthy inventor and firearm manufacturer. Like
his grandfather, Frampton is a hothead and is impatient with
many social institutions. He finds himself pitted against the
aristocratic fox-hunting set, who have little appreciation for
good art or for the goodness of the common man. Frampton's
fiancée Margaret, the moderating influence in his life, dies in
a car crash on the eve of their wedding. He brashly and
bitterly continues on alone, supporting young artists in pub-
lic-works projects and antagonizing the aristocrats. The story
has a generalized rather than a specific conflict and therefore
no particular climax. Mansell's life simply takes a turn for the
better when he falls in love with a ballet dancer, who happens
to be the dead Margaret's cousin. This book, and indeed all
of the Mansell books, manifests a characteristic weakness.
The stories dwell on the heroes' reverses and disappointments
at great length, and then suddenly, for no apparent reason,
everything works out for the best in a rushed and unlikely
conclusion.

Dead Ned (1938) and its companion piece *Live and
Kicking Ned* (1939) follow the same pattern of belabored
episodes and breathless endings. The earlier book is the better constructed of the two. A murder, a mistaken conviction,

and a recovery from death by hanging provide the reader with a large dose of action. The hero, Dr. Edward Mansell, is wrongly accused of the murder of his benefactor, Admiral Cringle. After being hanged, but not killed, he is given a new identity as a ship's doctor on a slave vessel. His adventures at sea and in the new world are taken up in *Live and Kicking Ned*, perhaps the dullest and most episodic of Masefield's novels.

By 1940 Masefield had had enough of the Mansell family and turned again to historical fiction. Although most of his novels are set in the past, he had never written about an important historical personage. He did so with great success in *Basilissa*, the story of Theodora, a dancer and courtesan, who rises to become the wife and counselor of the Emperor Justinian. Although she is Masefield's only female protagonist, Theodora is not an unfamiliar figure. A self-made woman who succeeds through her talents, intelligence, and personal attractiveness, she resembles several Masefield heroes, and indeed, Masefield himself. Like her creator, she suffers snubs because she lacks an upper-class pedigree, but in the end, she is accepted and royally rewarded. Masefield's double interest in the dance and in public speaking makes the book's theater scenes and political debates particularly lively.

The final two Masefield novels are hardly novels at all. *Conquer, A Tale of the Nika Rebellion* (1941) and *Badon Parchments* (1947) are short and undramatic narratives of events that occurred during the reign of Justinian and Theodora. The former takes place in Byzantium, the latter in Britain. Although Masefield's interest in the Byzantine Empire had not lessened, his powers as a novelist had. His lifelong fascination with the logistics of real battles spills over and mars his narratives. The stories of his last two novels have ossified into battle reports.

The novel was clearly not Masefield's genre. The task of sustaining a properly paced and complex narrative was difficult for him. His tendency was to belabor certain incidents and then rush through others. After his first few books, he dispensed with chapter divisions entirely. This quirk indicates that he did not build his narratives in developed units; instead he was content to let them expand. He also became too fond of enumerating preparations and procedures. Descriptions of setting up a camp, or of rigging a ship, or of issuing provisions play too prominent a role in his narration. Oddly enough, his fussiness over detail and care for the arrangement of the physical world did not transfer into a professional fastidiousness in the revision of his manuscripts.

Although Masefield is not always good with dialogue, he is a master of discussion. Almost every novel has a characteristic meeting where strategy is discussed and possibilities are tossed out and mulled over. This working out of options betrays Masefield's penchant for the methodical, but he is very good at phrasing argument and counter argument and has the ability to make the reader enter into the characters' minds.

Masefield's people are often types rather than individuals. More than once the reader meets the careful and sensitive working man, the arrogant aristocrat, the wise older woman. The heroes are too often without faults and the villains too often without graces. Women present a particular problem. There are so few of them: between *The Street of Today* (1911) and *Basilissa* (1940), there is never more than one important woman character per book. Often there are none at all. Although Masefield was clearly sensitive and sympathetic to women, he seems to have consciously stopped trying to dramatize their feelings. The love scenes he includes from time to time are weak and abbreviated. He may have avoided putting complicated women into his novels because they did not lend themselves to adventure stories. Their presence also added psychological and sexual elements that he did not wish to explore.

All of Masefield's novels, in the end, are about Masefield. They champion an aristocracy of the spirit rather than one of rank or birth. The hero, like Masefield, is always an adventurer or a working man—self-educated and eager to learn, rather than privileged and complacent. What seems to be the compulsory happy ending is not a sop to the readers but a further instance of Masefield's art following his life. If, after hardship, poverty, and hard work, he had achieved fame and happiness, then so might his heroes.

5

••

The Sonnets

It was inevitable that Masefield should write a book of sonnets, for several of the great writers of the past whom he considered his mentors were skillful sonneteers. Although he imitated these poets, Masefield was not like them. They were intellectual and he was not—nor did he wish to be. William Shakespeare, Sir Philip Sidney, and John Donne had the ability to translate knotty existential problems into evocative images. They were thinkers as well as masters of language. Because they dealt with complex problems in the rigidly structured sonnet form, they often turned to the shorthand of pun and paradox. Masefield had no use for such devices. He wrote well over a hundred sonnets during his career, but not one of them contains the intellectual fireworks associated with Shakespeare and Donne. Although he was a very intelligent and well-read man, Masefield consciously shied away from the overly complicated. One of his principal drives was to smooth out the crooked and simplify the difficult. When his sonnets succeed, they do so on his terms.

His first efforts, which appeared in *Ballads* (1903) and *Ballads and Poems* (1910), were hardly sonnets at all. They have fourteen lines and follow the rhyme scheme of the Shakespearean sonnet, but instead of being self-contained, they are loose and open-ended. For example, the 1903 poem "Born for Naught Else" begins each quatrain with the same phrase, a repetition that calls to mind a ballad rather than a sonnet. The reader is met with a piling-on of observation that could continue for several more verses. There is no sense of shift or contrast as the poem moves from octet to sestet.

"Born for Naught Else" is typical of the first Masefield sonnets. Six others appear in the early collections, each lacking the tightness and the intensity associated with the sonnet. Undistinguished word choice further dissipates Masefield's emotion. Adjectives like "dear," "little," "lovely," and "marvelous" make these first sonnets appear particularly flabby and lifeless. "The Death Rooms" alone shows promise of what is to come. In this poem, Masefield begins to use the sonnet to advantage. The openness of the speaker's emotion and the almost-confessional quality of the octet contrast sharply with the shame and the wish to hide his ugly past that is found in the sestet. Although the specters from the past are decaying, they will not disappear, and the poet visits them at night in dreams to learn again his bitter lesson. The conflict between visiting the past and trying to hide it, between seeing it decay and watching it glow, gives the sonnet an interesting tension.

Between 1910, when "The Death Rooms" was published, and 1916, when the *Sonnets* volume appeared, Masefield translated several Renaissance sonnets written by Spanish and Portuguese masters. These exercises clearly helped him understand the mechanics of the sonnet form and appreciate its possibilities as well as its limitations. The translations also challenged Masefield to use the more complicated Petrarchan rhyme scheme (*a b b a, a b b a, c d e, c d e*) over which he shows a competent mastery. When the time came, however, for him to write his own sequence, he returned to the Shakespearean form (*a b a b, c d c d, e f e f, g g*) probably because it was less demanding and more solidly rooted in the English language.

Most of the sonnets in the 1916 volume were written in 1914 after World War I had broken out but before Masefield had joined the war effort.[1] Only two of them refer specifically to the war. The others recreate a world without God, a world

where man is master and where Beauty is the lost ideal he
seeks. These sonnets yearn nostalgically for the peace and
beauty Masefield had known as a child. He optimistically
assumes that the perfection he once felt must still exist, and
that it will not forever elude the questing soul. Both the flow-
ering of modern science and the disappearance of organized
religion feed Masefield's idealistic humanism. Several of the
sonnets recall John Donne's "Anniversarie" poems (1612,
1613), and in particular his observation that "the new philos-
ophie calls all in doubt." Masefield, like Donne, avoids wring-
ing his hands in despair over changes in the world wrought by
science and war. Instead, he is alive to the many new stimuli
they have ushered in.

Masefield's vision in his sonnets is one of man be-
leaguered, but still lord of the world. The logical conclusion
of man's considerable power comes in the thirty-third sonnet
with the outright denial of God's existence. In His place,
Masefield elevates Beauty, the perfect bliss he knew as a child.
The nature of this Beauty, its link to the material world, and
its elusiveness are the themes that run through the sonnet
sequence. Sometimes Masefield is discouraged, and sometimes he sees hope for the future. The sequence ends with a
fatalism that celebrates life's persistence in a godless and ran-
dom universe.

Masefield's philosophy is not a complicated one and often generates mediocre sonnets. Still, a good number of his
efforts are interesting, and a few are truly masterful. His
musings on whether nature submits to the orderly self-govern-
ment that mankind so perversely resists are charmingly expressed in the twenty-eighth sonnet that begins,

> Is there a great green commonwealth of Thought
> Which ranks the yearly pageant, and decides
> How summer's royal progress shall be wrought,
> By secret stir which in each plant abides?

The metaphor of the human form of government at work in nature sits lightly on the poem. Even though the flowers belong to a commonwealth, Masefield makes certain that they are still recognizable as themselves. The commonwealth is a green one, and the daffodil still rocks characteristically in the spring breezes. The plants may decide, abide, consent, and agree, but they are still plants. Rather than humanizing the flowers, Masefield's images lend a kind of natural beauty to the idea of orderly and reasonable human government. The tentativeness of the questions also adds to the sweetness of the poem's tone. The final couplet undercuts the positive and consciously ordered quality of the natural world by introducing human beings:

> Or is it, as with us, unresting strife,
> And each consent a lucky gasp for life?

With the mention of man come words of discord and anxiety. The transformation of consent from a willing acquiescence to a "lucky gasp" jars the poem's tone and leaves the reader unexpectedly disturbed.

Masefield was by no means blind to nature's harsh side, and captures it forcefully in the twenty-fourth, twenty-fifth, and twenty-sixth sonnets. Although the first of these emphasizes the destructive power of animal predators and their impulse to kill, it does not pass judgment on them. Masefield calls these animals fierce and fearful, but not cruel; not consciously evil, they take "dumb joy" in their actions. The richness of this poem's vocabulary suggests Masefield's exultation in the vitality of these predators:

> There are two forms of life, of which one moves,
> Seeking its meat in many forms of Death,
> On scales, on wings, on all the myriad hooves
> Which stamp earth's exultation in quick breath.

> It rustles through the reeds in shivering fowl,
> Cries over moor in curlew, glitters green
> In the lynx's eye, is fearful in the howl
> Of winter-bitten wolves. . . .

The following two sonnets, neither of which is technically as fine as the first, link the animal predators with the human mind. Masefield sees the mind's fierceness as a virtue that enables man to expose misconceptions and bring the truth to light.

This sequence of three poems highlights Masefield's strengths and weaknesses as a sonneteer. His best sonnets, in general, are those like the first one; they do not attempt to explain too much. The more convoluted an idea becomes, the less successful Masefield is in imposing upon it the sonnet form. When he cannot telescope his message into fourteen lines, Masefield often allows himself to spill over into a second poem. The result is usually not a happy one: in place of one tightly argued poem, there are two loose ones. Each boasts three or four good lines, but the rest is not memorable.

More new sonnets appeared in Masefield's 1917 collection, *Lollingdon Downs and Other Poems*. Beauty is still the poet's polestar, but its link to the physical body is considerably more pronounced. Indeed, he seems almost fixated with words like "blood" and "brain" and "cell," which appear over and over again. One senses that Masefield is trying to distance himself from the horrors of war that he has now seen firsthand. He attempts to speak generally and philosophically, but he is too affected by the war experience to do so successfully. In the *Lollingdon Downs* sonnets, Masefield is not speaking philosophically; he is hiding behind philosophy, afraid to explore his own feelings of horror and despair. Not surprisingly, these poems are among his worst. Overly earnest, vague, and repetitive, they carry a hidden message of great pain.

The best of the *Lollingdon Downs* sonnets, "Is it a sea?" (XV) ventures to guess what death might be like. Because the theme forces the poet to search for metaphor, this sonnet avoids the abstractness and the generalities that mar so many of the others. With great specificity, Masefield relates death to what he knows. Perhaps death is like putting out to sea, or lighting up a dark house, or offering help to a friend, or sleeping. He does not relate death to human happiness or unearthly bliss. The sestet of the sonnet dwells on the sleep metaphor: death may be rest, a loss of humanity, and a melding with inanimate nature. Without mentioning the horrors of war in this sonnet, Masefield expresses his own fatigue and his desire for respite from mankind's folly. He sees death not as a perfection of what is good in man, but as a release from humanity altogether.

Although the *Lollingdon Downs* poems indicate a loosening of Masefield's grasp on the sonnet, he returned to the form after the war with renewed skill. Of particular interest is the short sonnet sequence called *Animula* that appeared in 1920. The twelve poems of *Animula* provide an evocative sketch of a love triangle between a beautiful young woman, her brilliant, but unfulfilled husband, and a scholar-poet who comes to live in their small town. Too short to be a narrative poem, and too cohesive and descriptive to be what is traditionally called a sonnet sequence, *Animula* is a curious hybrid. Most of the poems are descriptive: two provide a look at the setting; three introduce the principal characters; and another three, toward the end, describe the death of those characters. The last and weakest of the sonnets attempts to moralize the tragedy and bring "sweet from bitter things." Only the three middle sonnets discuss what actually happens between the characters. By downplaying the action, Masefield suggests its inevitability. The small-town setting and the three character types are all that is necessary for this tragic equation.

Masefield is at his best when describing the tormented husband:

> A grand man, with a beauty and a pride,
> A manner and a power and a fire
> With beaks of vultures eating at his side,
> The great brain mad with unfulfilled desire.

One townsman sees him as

> an unused force and [his wife] a child.
> She caught him with her beauty, being a maid.
> The thought that she had trapped him drove him wild.

His death, coming long years after his unhappy wife has drowned herself, is a fitting complement to his life:

> All through his life his will had kennelled him,
> Now he was free, and with a hackling fell
> He snarled out of the body to the dim
> To run the spirits with the hounds of hell.
> To run forever at the quarry gone,
> The uncaught thing a little farther on.

The metaphor of the husband's soul as a kenneled hound captures the frustration with which he lived his life. The extension of the metaphor so that in death his soul joins the hounds of hell jarringly negates the unhappy man's hope for release. Death has not freed him; it has merely introduced him into a larger prison, a greater frustration. The final couplet recalls the opening lines. In the husband's raving to "beat the hound," one sees that he unknowingly speaks of himself. He is, as the poem's imagery makes clear, both dog and master, and as such he is responsible for the torture of his own life. It is he who has caged and beaten his own soul. The several repetitions of the words "out" and "run" mock the longed-for freedom that he never finds.

Animula shows Masefield warring with the sonnet form, unconsciously insisting that he is a storyteller and not a sonneteer. He is both; he may not have been comfortable writing sonnets, but he had the ability. The best proof of his sonnet-writing skill appears in the same year as *Animula* in the *Enslaved* volume. "The Lemmings," "Forget," and two sonnets "On Growing Old" are often anthologized, and they deserve to be. "The Lemmings" in particular shows that Masefield was capable of rising above the bland and the general without the vehicle of a story to sustain him. The unusual metaphor of men as lemmings lends an interesting texture to the theme that so haunted Masefield—the quest for ideal Beauty in the fallen world. The first quatrain, through the insistent repetition of the word "westward," evokes the trance-like march of the lemmings to their death as they search for food. Though Masefield bluntly says of the lemmings that the sea "drowns them dumb," he transforms them in the second quatrain from mindless creatures into intelligent beings seeking a shelter and a land of plenty that once existed. The sestet then compares man's search for the spiritual food of God's quiet to the lemmings' quest for sustenance. The power of these last six lines lies in the quiet nostalgia of the third quatrain that is undercut sharply and sadly by the final couplet's denial of success. One reason this sonnet works so well is that Masefield avoids ponderous abstractions. The message is hardly different from that in any number of the less-successful Beauty sonnets in the 1916 collection. Here, however, Masefield anchors Beauty to a specific object—a human face. Use of the word "westward" in six of the fourteen lines adds a haunting and distressing quality to the poem, as the meaning of the word shifts from death, to hope, and back to death again.

"On Growing Old," perhaps Masefield's best-known sonnet, conveys a more mellow sadness:

> Be with me Beauty, for the fire is dying,
> My dog and I are old, too old for roving.
> Man, whose young passion sets the spindrift flying,
> Is soon too lame to march, too cold for loving.

The fire metaphor of the first line, to which Masefield returns in the final couplet, sets the tone of the poem. Although the speaker is melancholy that he is old, he is also philosophical, recognizing that there is a special beauty in memory, just as there is a special beauty in the embers of a dying fire. The inanimate objects around him—the yellowed leaves of the book, the ticking clock, the withered wire in the spinet—all suggest his own aging body. Nevertheless, the tone is so calm that, instead of chastening the poet, these objects provide him with a harmonious backdrop. The pastoral landscape in the third quatrain, with the romantic image of the knight rallying the broken squadron, is not an evocation of another world. Rather, it is the youthful equivalent of sitting by the fire. The tone is the same—calm and uncomplaining. The right-acting knight rallies his squadron as the right-thinking poet masters his thoughts. A kind of harmony pervades the poem to suggest that Beauty is indeed "with" the speaker and probably always has been.

Masefield never wholly abandoned writing sonnets, but after 1920 they appear singly, rather than in sequences. The critics may have discouraged him, for they came down harder on his sonnets than on most of his other work. A common and valid complaint is that the Masefield sonnet bears its burden of thought with difficulty. It is intriguing to wonder whether a university education would not have equipped Masefield with more of the discipline and the patience necessary for sonnet writing. As it is, he has written a handful of first-rate sonnets: he might have produced dozens.

6

◆◆

The Plays

The plays are the undiscovered treasures of the Masefield canon. They never received the recognition they deserved, a fact that discouraged Masefield and probably inhibited him from writing more dramatic literature. As it is, he wrote ten prose plays and six in verse, composed during the four decades between 1909 and 1948. None of them enjoyed long runs in London. Some were staged in smaller towns, and others were performed at the Masefields' Music Room theater in Oxford.

In many ways the drama was a hospitable medium for Masefield's talent. He had a good ear for dialogue and a particular facility for capturing the nuances of argument and discussion. Furthermore, a play's length limitation served as a useful curb on his tendency to expand. Masefield was well aware of this built-in discipline: "To a story teller, interested in all ways of the telling of tales, a play is nothing but a story in its simplest form. . . . To practice the intense condensation necessary in dramatic writing, to reduce a fable to its simplest terms, and keep it simple and poignant for an hour or two hours, is helpful exercise to any story teller."[1]

Masefield's interest in writing drama began in 1900 with his exposure to the Yeats circle. Both Yeats and Lady Gregory were busily engaged in writing plays in verse and prose about the Irish peasants. Masefield's close friendship with the brilliant young playwright John Synge, whom he met at Yeats's house, was an additional spur to his interest in the drama. The bluntness, the humor, and the peasant dialect of Masefield's early plays all betray Synge's influence. Even the introduction to *The Tragedy of Nan and Other Plays* (1909) echoes Synge's 1907 introduction to *The Playboy of the Western World*.

Masefield's first dramatic effort, *The Camden Wonder* (1905), tells the shocking story of John Perry, who falsely incriminates his hardworking brother Dick, his mother, and himself for the murder of a Mr. Harrison. The supposed victim is not dead at all but hiding out in another town. The notion that a man would willingly bring about his own death in order to have his mother and brother executed is both appalling and intriguing. Masefield did not invent the story but based it on a fable he had heard in Camden. John, whose character owes something to Shakespeare's Iago, delights in the evil that he is doing. When he "confesses" the murder, he insists that someone be there to write it down. He imaginatively seizes on the unexpected when it occurs and turns it to his evil purpose. When a hair net falls out of Dick's pocket during the arrest, John quickly says it was used to strangle the victim. As the execution hour draws near, John amuses himself by imagining the ballads that will be composed about himself and his family.

The Camden Wonder explores in a brief and intense way the depth of human evil and the ineptitude of the well-meaning law. Of course the action is, as some critics complained, improbable. It is nevertheless riveting and thought provoking, touching on a deep psychological truth about people's perverse capacity for evil.

Mrs. Harrison continues *The Camden Wonder* story. Although less satisfying than its predecessor, it is still an interesting short play. When the title character, the wife of the supposedly dead man, finds out that her husband was paid to go away, she is stunned. He, in contrast, remains unmoved by the enormity of what he has done. He threatens to kill his wife if she tells the authorities what really happened. The play becomes briefly comic when the inept Harrison cannot manufacture a plausible lie for the parson who comes to inquire about the particulars of his disappearance. In the end, however, Harrison's callousness interferes with the success of the play. Masefield chose to emphasize Mrs. Harrison's reaction to the evil deed, rather than to explore her husband's indifference to it. The audience is left wishing that the author had probed more into Harrison's perplexing lack of concern and less into his wife's understandable despair.

The Tragedy of Nan (1908), Masefield's first full-length drama, is a kind of Cinderella story with a tragic ending. Nan, whose father has been hanged for stealing a sheep, lives with her aunt and uncle, the Pargetters. Mr. Pargetter is kindly enough, but his wife and daughter Jenny are jealous and mean-spirited, constantly working to discredit and humiliate Nan. The witchlike guardian is not an unfamiliar figure in Masefield's work and probably owes something to his stern and unloving Aunt Kate.

The play's characters fall into two categories. On one side are Nan and an old, blind fiddler called the Gaffer. Both remain faithful to those they love, despite what society may think of their loved ones or of their devotion. On the other side are Jenny, Mrs. Pargetter, and Dick, a young man who loves Nan but refuses to marry her when he finds out her father was a criminal. In the end, Masefield singles out Dick as the most dangerous of all the characters because he is weak. When Nan's father's name is cleared and she receives reparation money, Dick again asserts his love for her. She tests him and says she will give away the money. Immediately, he reneges. Furious at his weakness and heartbroken that her father has died for a crime he did not commit, Nan stabs Dick with a pastry knife and drowns herself.

Although the plot is sentimental and extreme, Masefield

makes it credible through his evocation of the world the peasants inhabit. Conversations about old age and the sad fate of country women after they marry and bear children anchor the characters in a harsh, but recognizable environment. Even Dick's complaints about his inability to support a family without some dowry from his wife elicits sympathy from the audience.

The Tragedy of Nan was dedicated to Yeats and it clearly suggests his influence. The peasant dialect, the subject matter, and the prophetic ability of the blind Gaffer all seem particularly Yeatsian. The introduction's uncharacteristically pompous references to "commonplace people [who] cannot suffer and cannot exult" may also have been a bit of snobbery that Masefield picked up from Yeats. Despite the tone of the introduction, the play itself rings true. It is among Masefield's best dramas, a remarkable accomplishment when one remembers that it was the author's first full-length play.

The Sweeps of Ninety-Eight and The Locked Chest were published together in 1916 but written a decade earlier in 1906. Both are one-act comedies, similar in tone to those Lady Gregory was writing at the time and probably influenced by her. The Sweeps is set in Ireland right after the unsuccessful 1798 uprising at Killala. The hero, Irish rebel leader Tiger Roche, is about to escape to France, but before doing so, he manages to make fools of several British officers by, among other things, stuffing them up a chimney. Masefield explained that most of the improbable incidents in the play were his invention, but that two of the characters "once lived and used some of the words allotted to them."[2]

The British officers in The Sweeps appear almost too loutish to be believed. They find hangings a cause for hilarity, and when Roche says he is reading The Odes of Horace, one of them boorishly comments, "I know that Odes O'Horace to be a pamphleteering rebel." Masefield's having spent time with several Irish authors gave him a new perspective on Irish history. He was plainly embarrassed by his country's insensitivity to Irish problems, and *The Sweeps* serves as his personal apology to his friends.

The Locked Chest is more finely drawn than *The Sweeps of Ninety-Eight*, and all its characters are thoroughly believable. Based on a story from the Icelandic *Laxdael* saga, it dramatizes the age-old conflict between family loyalty and the forces of law. Vigdis, an agreeable and spirited peasant woman, is yoked to a grumpy and weak-principled old man named Thord. When her cousin Thorolf accidentally kills a man in a fight, Thord fears retaliation and refuses to protect him. Thorolf explains that the incident was provoked, and Vigdis accepts the death matter-of-factly, saying, "I'm not blaming you, Thorolf. It seems that men must kill each other from time to time."

Thord's cowardice becomes humorous as he cringes before Ingiald, the dead man's brother. Unable to dissemble, he quickly succumbs to Ingiald's offer of a bribe. Vigdis discovers the money, and through her own courage and her shrewd perception of human nature, she outsmarts both Ingiald and her husband. Disgusted by Thord's weakness, she departs with Thorolf, leaving her husband to fend for himself.

The Faithful, written in 1913, is the tale of two Japanese knights, Asano and Kurano, whose lands are confiscated by an unscrupulous rival. Although the play's focus blurs somewhat as the action shifts from Asano in act one to Kurano in the final two acts, it still impresses the audience. Masefield captures the discipline of the Japanese nobles' lives and successfully imitates the careful understatement of Japanese verse. Being set in Japan, *The Faithful* would seem to be a step away from Yeats and his circle, but it is not. Yeats had a strong interest in Japanese No drama and probably was the one to steer Masefield in this direction. The cadences of the speeches in the play, especially in the second act when a number of Japanese soldiers speak of their hardships, also recall moments in many of Yeats's tragedies. In general, members of the Yeats circle were a good influence on Masefield's dramatic talents. Synge's untimely death in 1909 and the outbreak of World War I a few years later severed the connection. However, even in the early twenties, the influence was not entirely gone.

Melloney Holtspur (1922), for instance, still shows evidence of Yeats's hold on Masefield's imagination. In true Yeatsian tradition, spirits play an important role in the drama. Indeed the two main characters, Melloney Holtspur and Lonnie Copshrewes, are already dead as the play opens. In life, Melloney had rejected Lonnie, owing to some flaws in his character. Both die young and unhappy, she without ever marrying and he having entered into a loveless union.

Masefield's sympathies lie with Lonnie, a talented artist who cannot satisfy both his art and the woman he loves. Although he has behaved badly on several occasions, Lonnie is sorry for his misdeeds and, in the end, he is driven to repay those whom he has wronged. His deep concern for his work echoes Masefield's own insecurities: "Do you think I care for this green earth? I don't. I've put to sea from it, and my art's my boat, and the sea's rough and the boat's leaky. Worried about my work? I've given my soul for it, and after all, it isn't good, it isn't good."

In contrast to Lonnie, Melloney is virtuous, but she cannot forgive him for his wildness and his human weakness. In death she becomes vindictive and admits she enjoys seeing her lover suffer. Bitter and cruel, as the self-righteous often are, Melloney attempts to destroy both Lonnie's paintings and his daughter's happiness. Yet she is not always unsympathetic. On several occasions she is heard singing "Plaisirs d'Amour," and then her sufferings seem very real.

Lonnie's daughter Lenda is the play's most balanced character. Like Masefield's Nan, she remains faithful to her father's memory and proud of his talent. Neither jealous nor resentful, she, unlike Melloney, is willing to forgive. When she describes her father's life, it sounds like a version of Masefield's own:

He was weak, he was wicked; very wicked if you like. I should not wonder. From the time he was born he had no help, no guidance; nothing was done for him, nothing was smoothed for him. He fought and suffered from boyhood on. In spite of all that, he was one of the best painters of his time.

Melloney Holtspur is Masefield's last drama written totally in prose and his last drama about ordinary people. He had composed three verse plays before 1922, but he seems to have felt more comfortable during the early years working in prose. As a group, Masefield's verse plays are markedly inferior to the prose ones. The fault, one suspects, lies not in the medium, but in the subject matter. Masefield explained in 1925 that verse drama should deal with "the Gods, the elements, the soul of man, and the fables of a nation." He dismissed "accidents and incidents of personality" as inappropriate to dramatic poetry, saying that the aim of verse drama was to show "the heart of life as it is displayed at great moments."[3] He deviated from his guidelines only once, in 1925, with *The Trial of Jesus*, a drama containing some verse but written mostly in prose. Although the play is supposed to be realistic (hence the prose), it never catches fire. The prose is pedestrian and the verse often doggerel. Jesus' last speech contains this embarrassing couplet:

> I am the man ye scourged and slew
> I hang from the tree ye nailed me to.

Masefield had difficulty both in verse and prose when he wrote dramas about great people and great moments. He was at his best with those very subjects that he excluded from the province of verse drama. His six verse dramas concern themselves not with "accidents and incidents" of the common people but with biblical, historical, and legendary figures.

Pompey the Great (1908) is Masefield's first play in verse. Leaving the peasants and the familiar countryside, the author moves into the imaginative landscape of Ancient Rome where tragedy unfolds against a grand backdrop and the hero is one of history's luminaries instead of a common man. One can understand Masefield's fascination with the thoughtful patrician Gnaeus Pompeius Magnus, who lost power to the more aggressive and practical Julius Caesar. Masefield no doubt saw part of his own philosophy mirrored in Pompey's humane and high-minded patriotism. He does not, however, idealize the noble Roman, who often appears indecisive and impractical.

Although the play has some fine moments, its time span is too great and its view too detailed. The pace is slowed by an overload of political information and a number of very long speeches. Furthermore, certain phrases like "all in the same boat" and "cooped up" seem oddly inappropriate to the play's elevated tone. In the end, Masefield's wish to write fine speeches for the noble hero interferes with the amount of action in the drama. In his native plays where the characters are simple men and women, Masefield uses long speeches sparingly because they are inappropriate to their speakers. He allows eloquence only at moments of strong emotion. In *Pompey*, with greater men and greater leeway, he is less adept, and the play seems bloated.

Philip the King (1914) relies on the technique of having the main character react to events that occur offstage. King Philip II of Spain and his daughter worry about, dream about, and finally learn the sad truth about the fate of the Spanish Armada. Their reactions often seem wooden and lacking in power. Too much history is related secondhand and too little emotion comes through. As Philip is told of his fleet's devastation, he does little more than ask leading questions of the messenger. Here, as in several other Masefield works, the author's interest in military and naval history dampens his literary sensibility. *Philip the King* lacks drama because it is a play without conflict. It comes across as a slice from the end of a Greek tragedy. A great man is brought low, but the audience is robbed of all that went before.

Good Friday (1916), the earliest of Masefield's three verse plays on the life of Christ, is interesting, but like *Philip the King*, it uses the technique of history retold through the eyes of secondary characters. Christ never appears on stage and so the conflict is reduced to a difference of opinion between Pilate and his wife Procula. She understands that killing Jesus would be a mistake, but her husband allows events to carry him along despite his reservations. Like Nan's suitor Dick in *The Tragedy of Nan*, Pilate lacks both vision and strength of character.

The Coming of Christ (1928) and *Easter* (1929) seem liturgical rather than dramatic. In the former, the Christmas story is retold and Masefield unwittingly finds himself competing with the King James translation of the Bible. Few poets have succeeded in that endeavor. The latter play contains one interesting invention, a character called The Way of the World, who speaks some arresting lyric lines of philosophical poetry. One understands that although Masefield called these last two works dramas, they were not dramas in the traditional sense and he did not expect them to be judged by traditional standards.

In between *Good Friday* and *The Coming of Christ*, Masefield composed two other verse plays. The first, *A King's Daughter* (1923), is a blank verse tragedy in five acts, linking the fate of the biblical Jezebel to that of Helen of Troy. Each act concludes with speeches on the life of Helen, which seem strangely out of place in the story of the pagan queen Jezebel's maneuverings in the kingdom of Israel. Masefield

fails to demonstrate clearly what it is that Helen and Jezebel
have in common and the reader is perplexed by the experiment of yoking the two distinct stories. A reviewer for the
Times Literary Supplement accurately called the play "curious" and "strange" and concluded, "This tragedy will hardly
add to Mr. Masefield's reputation."[4]

Four years later Masefield tried another experiment, a
dramatization of the legend of Tristram and Isolde. The major difficulty was to select which of the many episodes of the
legend to include. Unable to ignore several of the major incidents, Masefield chose to mention them all briefly before
settling down to tell the tale of the lovers' final meeting. After
Tristan and Isolt Masefield quickly realized that, because of
their complexity, medieval legends do not lend themselves to
the stage. In the following years he was to use narrative instead of dramatic verse for such stories.

When he became Poet Laureate, Masefield virtually
ceased to write drama. He composed only two more short
pieces, *The End and Beginning* (1933) about Mary, Queen of
Scots, and much later, *A Play of St. George* (1948). The
unenthusiastic critical reception to his postwar drama cou-
pled with his own sense of his new position deterred him from
writing again for the stage. Taken as a whole, Masefield's
dramatic oeuvre is extremely varied. He was ambitious to a
fault in what he was willing to try. At least in the beginning,
he was very happy as a dramatist. Reminiscing in 1925, he
said, "I was a playwright, according to my power, for ten
years. . . . We did not do what we hoped to do (the war
stopped that), but we had good fun in trying, and the sport of
the effort, mixed up, as it was, with the beauty of youth and
the depth of friendship, seems now some of the salt of my
life."[5]

During the twenties Masefield carried his love of the
drama into the production of amateur theatricals at the Music Room. There his own plays, as well as those by Shake-

speare, Yeats, Lady Gregory, and many others, were staged. Masefield had both the desire and the talent to have pursued playwriting more single-mindedly than he did. What he lacked was the thick skin necessary to withstand the immediate criticism that new plays must always receive. Talented though he was, Masefield backed away from playwriting and instead devoted himself to his novels and poems.

7

◆◆◆

The Best of the
Laureateship Poems

Even Masefield's greatest admirers are dismayed by the quality of his poetry after he became Poet Laureate in 1930. Although he continued to be staggeringly prolific, everyone seems to agree that little of this later work is memorable. Understandably, the average reader is not willing to wade through so much material in order to find a handful of good poems; even a Masefield devotee becomes discouraged. This is unfortunate, for in his thirty-seven years as Poet Laureate, Masefield did write a number of very fine poems — enough to fill a thin volume and aid in the revival of a dying reputation. Some critics might object that a poet who wrote so much mediocre poetry does not deserve editing on such a grand scale, and there is some merit in this objection. The aim of this chapter is not to falsify Masefield's reputation as Poet Laureate, but instead to bring to light some sensitive and affecting poems that have been completely ignored.

Between the years 1930 and 1967, Poet Laureate John Masefield brought out eighteen volumes of poetry. Some, like *Land Workers* (1942), are little more than pamphlets containing a single poem. Others, like *The Country Scene* (1937), came out in deluxe folios with original artwork accompanying every poem. The remainder are traditional collections of lyric and narrative verse, sometimes running more than two hundred pages. When the best poems are winnowed out and read as a collection, they produce a startling effect, for they enhance one another and elevate considerably the reader's assessment of Masefield's late verse.

The success of these poems generally depends on the formula of simple diction, subdued emotion, and an intricate rhyme scheme. It was not easy for a man with the elevated title of Poet Laureate to write according to such a formula, especially if he takes his job as seriously as Masefield did. Avoidance of inflated, archaic diction was probably the hardest task for Masefield, for he had always been partial to words and expressions like "oft" and "full many." The more successful he became, the farther he drifted from the direct and simple voice he had used in his early *Salt-Water Ballads*. Even when he wrote about nature, his verse was often weighted down by abstractions and history. It is a surprise and a relief, then, to find buried in his late verse several nature poems whose scope is modest and whose words are simple.

"The Gulls upon the Saltings" (*The Country Scene*) shows that Masefield still had the ability to observe life closely:

> They mew above the boilings in the wake
> Eyeing the million bubbles for a prize;
> They lean upon the roarings of the skies;
> All the sea's soul is in the cry they make.
> They have seen the colors of all Nations shake
> In ships at sea; but here they stand at dreams,
> One-legged on mud flats where the salting gleams.

Masefield evokes the life of a gull in its turbulence and quietness without comment or heavy generalizing. Driven by hunger and the winds, the gulls see the evidence of men's political divisions, but are not moved. Human preoccupations, which often seem so important, are put into another perspective as the reader observes the gulls.

Like his lyrics, Masefield's best short narratives of this period succeed because of their simplicity of diction. Two poems in particular, "Jouncer's Tump" (*On the Hill*, 1949) and "The Towerer" (*A Letter from Pontus*, 1936), are appealing because of the simple and direct voices of their narrators. When Masefield brings the English peasant into his poetry, he often idealizes or romanticizes him. However, the peasant narrators in these poems are not types; they are flawed and interesting individuals. The speaker in "Jouncer's Tump," a bored soldier home from the wars, convinces a drinking companion to help him dig into Jouncer's Tump, an ancient burial mound that is reputed to house a hoard of gold. They find treasure there in the form of a golden coat of mail. Awed, but more strongly driven by greed, they seize the armor and quickly melt it down. Unexpectedly, the narrator chances upon one link of the mail that has escaped melting. To his amazement, he is moved by the beauty of the piece and the skill with which it was wrought:

> It was a coin, or link, or flake,
> Stamped with an ear of corn,
> A marvel of an ancient make
> By men of heretoforn . . .
> None recent-born.
>
> None for a thousand years or two
> Had had the skill to leave
> That golden corn-ear done so due,
> From some long-mouldering sheave.
> It made me grieve.
>
> That neither of us once had seen
> That mail with any care;
> That neither knew what it had been

Nor what its beauties were
That we laid bare.

All of the coat, for all I knew
Had once been subtly wrought
Of links each beautiful and new
Like this one, (as I thought)
And now was nought.

The interesting half line at each stanza's end suggests a
thoughtful pause in the narrator's speech. The large number
of one-syllable words furthers the impression of his straightforwardness and makes his self-rebuke more touching. When
their vandalism is discovered, the two men are made to sur-
render the gold and repair the mound. Soon the crime recedes
in everyone's mind—everyone's but the narrator's. Neither
angry nor bitter, he carries with him a sense of wonder:

But two strange things there be; the one
That that lone golden link
That I had saved, was somehow gone
Through chance or theft or chink,
Where, I can't think.

The other, that my grand-dad told
Full forty years ago,
About the hero wrapped in gold
That we discovered so.
How did he know?

For he had never searched the mound;
None had, the scholars showed,
Since first the king went underground,
And Jouncer's Tump was strowed,
For his abode.

And scholars said the golden King
By what might still appear,

Had slumbered there a little thing
Of twice a thousand year,
Or very near.

And how my grand-dad knew that fact,
As fact we proved it be,
Two thousand years after the act,
Not any man can see.
It staggers me.

The engagement of the narrator's imagination is a rebuke to
the reader as well—have the sophisticated readers of this poem the sensitivity of this simple man?

Having chosen a peasant for his first-person narrator in
"Jouncer's Tump," Masefield is stylistically barred from elevated diction and abstract theorizing. The same limitations
are in place in "The Towerer." Here the crime committed is
less severe. The peasant narrator begins by telling of a day of
hunting:

Old Jarge, Hal, Walter and I, the Rector and Bill,
The old red setter and Joe, the retriever, Bess,
Went out in the cider time for something to kill,
Past Arthur's Camp, a couple of miles, I guess.

We came in the noon of the blue September day
To a tongue of grass thrust into a cleft of copse,
Berries were plump and black on the changing spray,
A dwindled spring went over its lip in drops.

The intentions of the hunting party contrast sharply with the
picture of fecund nature, but the narrator, being a plain man,
does not stop to comment. He simply goes on, remarking the
fate of one badly wounded partridge who struggles fiercely to
hold onto its life. With the passing years, the narrator gains
some perspective. Most of his hunting companions are dead,

and life has become more precious to him. In contrast to the natural deaths of his friends, the killing of the partridge now seems a crime—an unnatural act:

> Only Hal and myself of the nine remain,
> And Hal's forgotten the bird, forgotten the shoot;
> The grass, the wood and the spring are here in my brain,
> With the dogs and the wine-leaved brambles black with
>   fruit.

> I think of the towering bird with its choking lung,
> Its bursting heart, its struggle to scale the sky,
> And wonder when we shall all be tried and hung
> For the blue September crime when we made it die.

The beauty of these last verses lies in their easy comment on the casual lines of the beginning where the narrator openly states that he and his friends "went out in the cider time for something to kill." Like the narrator in "Jouncer's Tump," the speaker is not a thinking man; his focus is narrow and his diction, concrete. However, when he is struck by an idea, it is these very qualities that make his sense of wonder and his sense of guilt affecting.

Just as Masefield had to be careful with overly elevated diction, he also needed to check himself when tempted to write with inflated emotion. Those Masefield poems bursting with national pride or uplifting sentiment tend to say too much too simply. Poems that deal with only a subtle shift in tone or that cast only a glancing look at a large emotion succeed best for him. "Gipsies in the Snow" (*The Country Scene*) is such a poem:

> The bitter evening falls, the fog's about
> The horses droop and steam, the fire falls,

> The gipsies huddle, blowing on their nails,
> The Cold, the Enemy of Life, assails,
> Life, the humped bison, bows to keep him out.

The arresting image of life as a bison bowed to the cold opens the poem to make a statement on adversity. The animals, the fire, and the people all diminish themselves—bow to adversity—in order to survive. The poet suggests simply that man is part of nature and survives when he learns from nature. Adversity is a broad topic, and Masefield sometimes treated it sentimentally; but in "Gipsies in the Snow" it is modestly concentrated in the bison metaphor.

Solace gained from nature is a theme to which Masefield often returned. At the very end of his life, in his last collection of poems (*In Glad Thanksgiving*, 1967), he speaks touchingly about a particular hill that he sees as haunted by a spirit who has been his comrade since he was a boy. The theme of the poem recalls Wordsworth's "Tintern Abbey," and the third stanza even repeats a phrase from the last line of the Wordsworth poem. Although Masefield's diction totters on the verge of the overblown with words like "yon" and "of old," the strength of the feeling is clear, especially in the last two stanzas:

> O miracle of earthly joy
> Since before life began
> Who comforted a broken boy,
> And stanched a broken man.
>
> Take what of blessing age can give
> O marvel vast and dumb,
> And, O, be with me while I live
> And mine through what's to come.
>   ("The Hill")

The spirit is both god and friend to the elderly poet, and he looks to become one with it when he dies. Nature, not man, brings Masefield solace, and this poem is his hymn to it.

Like "The Hill," many of the later poems are sparked by memory. Some are self-indulgent and heavy-handed, but others like "The Flowing of the Sangarios" (*A Letter from Pontus*) use memory in an unpredictable and imaginative way. In the Sangarios poem, Masefield is traveling through the war-ravaged Turkish countryside when he begins to think, not of man's inhumanity to man, but of what had happened there so many centuries ago when Priam was King of Troy. He recalls Priam's story without bitterness, dwelling on the king's good fortune, and appreciating Zeus's kindness in sparing him foreknowledge of his life's unhappy end:

> I saw the sullen little river swerve
> Across the angry barren as we sped.
> The land was skinned down to the naked nerve,
> The war had blasted all the dwellers dead.
> No building near but had its roofing spilled
> Bare to the iron heaven overhead.
> Grey-brown the world was without touch of spring;
> The trees, the flowers and the grass were killed.
>
> To me that landscape was a wondrous thing.
>
> For once, in youth, King Priam, clad in bronze
> Marched by that river with the lads of Troy,
> Northward to battle with the Amazons;
> And having conquered them, retrod his track,
> Bearing his prize; there Hecuba and he
> Courted and wedded and begat their boy;
> Zeus in his mercy letting neither see
> The things he stewarded and meant to be: —
> Helen, the busy beaches, the attack;
> Skamander's water lilies red with blood;

> Achilles dragging Hector in the mud;
> The murder in the midnight and the sack.

The juxtaposition of harshness with wonder and happiness broadens the poem's scope without the use of grandiose diction. The title, with the image of the river, suggests the flow of time and puts even major upheavals like World War I and the Trojan War into perspective. Masefield's reaction is not horror but wonder at the way life unfolds. Skillfully, he isolates his own response in a single line between the poem's two descriptive passages. In so doing, he keeps his own feelings in perspective, too.

Although Masefield's poetry often deals with tragedy, it is rarely negative, and is infrequently concerned with fear, or cruelty, or depression. But when he does write about such things, the results are often impressive. Perhaps the best of his poems on soldiers' lives during World War II deals with fear. In "Sentries" (*A Generation Risen*, 1942) the poet observes that both men and animals hunt at night, leaving those who watch confused as to which predator's sounds they hear:

> Throughout the night, they stare into the dark
> For what in any darkness may be here,
> As silently as any snake or shark
> As deadly as the Sister with the shear.
> Alert, in eye and ear,
> They judge the ripple and the fox's bark.
>
> They wonder if the mist now wreathing-in
> Be filled with shapes as silent and as grey
> Or what, beyond there, made the dogs begin,
> And why the water splashed so in the bay,
> What death's essay
> Made that unseen hare scurry on the whin.
>
> They watch, they wonder, as in other years
> In other wars, men stared into the night

> For step or whisper of the men with spears
> Or padding of the wolf before the light,
> The east grows white.
> Another night is over with its fears.

Although the scene is rendered with immediacy, the story is an old one. The sentries are comrades of both nature's prey and of soldiers who stood sentry in other wars. The half line near the end of each stanza suggests a catching of the breath in response to an unfamiliar sound. Masefield maintains the intensity of the poem by keeping its scope small: relief comes not at the end of the war, but with the end of each night.

Another uncharacteristic emotion for a Masefield poem is the hard melancholy that pervades "The Mare and Foal at Grass" (*The Country Scene*). The theme of youth's careless innocence and the cruel constrictions of age is common to many poets, but rare in Masefield—perhaps because his life unfolded in the opposite way. He states here that both nature and man work to inhibit freedoms that the young take blithely for granted:

> Now that the grass is at its best in May,
> Before the gadfly with the jewelled eyes
> Lights on soft foot, for blood, the mare and foal
> Enjoy the sun's returning from the South,
> The swallow's darting and the cuckoo's toll.
>
> The young life gallops in his holiday,
> Destiny being dim and youth unwise.
> Still distant are the switches on his thighs
> And iron on his feet and in his mouth.

Both nature and man will soon close in on the foal's carefree existence. The odd pattern of the poem's rhymes (*a b c d c, a b b d*) mimics the foal's life by giving the lines a quality of false openness. At first, the poem seems to be written in blank verse; then, quite unexpectedly, rhyme appears and tightens up the structure. In a similar way, the foal's freedom is curbed.

If some of Masefield's late poems are surprisingly negative, a few others are delightfully fanciful. "The Bellringers" (*A Letter from Pontus*) brims with magic:

> What do they do, when all the ropes are still,
> When silence creeps again into her bower,
> When the stunned air is quick from its thrill,
> And he, who bears the lantern, locks the tower?
>
> Go home you say? I think the moonlight sees
> Those birds of sound that they have magicked near
> Bear them between their wings over the trees
> Through all the starways of the moon's career,
>
> Up, up, above the sparkless chimney cocks,
> Over the wildwood and away, away
> To where strange palace doors undo their locks,
> And waiting queens have secret things to say.

In an ideal world, a magic world, the maker of music would always have the royal ear. Using the tone he reserves for his children's books, Masefield fantasizes playfully on what the life of an artist should be like. Most of the time, he avoids whimsy in his lyric poetry, but here he lets down his guard.

The best poems of Masefield's late period are short and intricately rhymed. He had often used complicated rhyme schemes in his early narrative verse, but the length of these poems tended to defeat the discipline of the verse forms. He was less tempted by wordiness in his short poems. As a result, many of Masefield's intricately rhymed short poems are nicely spare and succinct. "February Night" (*A Letter from Pontus*) is a good example:

I went into the land where Beauty dwells.
The winter darkness shut it as a prison.
The thin moon, due at midnight, had not risen.
The clouds moved slowly over: nothing else
Stirred, nor did owl cry, nor did glow-worm glisten.
The night in all her vastness stood to listen.
Then, in the valley church, men rang the bells.

Out of the tower into the winter air
They shook their triumph: and a hill beyond
Made laggard ghosts of echoes to respond.
As turbulent water beats the boulder bare
And hurries and leaps, so turbulent drin and drone
Clanged and were spilled in cataracts of tone
Out of the tower above the ringers there.

Then the bells ceased; the men, as I suppose
Muffling their throats in woollens, trudged to bed.
The heaven displayed her star-work overhead
Star beyond star, the brighter as it froze.
A fox barked thrice, none answered, the world slept,
Save at some oven where a cricket kept
Trilling the drowsy cat into a doze.

The first stanza pictures a world still with anticipation. The moon, the animals, Beauty itself—all await the signal that wakes the night world into life. The arresting metaphor of the ringing bells as turbulent water spilling in "cataracts of tone" dominates the second stanza. As the ringing ceases, the midnight comes to life—not wildly, but softly and sporadically. The clouds of the first verse have disappeared and the stars are out. The bells have liberated the prison of winter darkness. The interesting rhyme scheme (*a b b a c c a*) lends the poem a subtle framework and provides a check on the wildness of the ringing bells. The intensity of the sound, like the intensity of all art, can wake up a sleeping world and make it move—if only slightly.

A more conventional poetic form, the Petrarchan sonnet, is used masterfully by Masefield in "The Waggon-Maker" (*A Letter from Pontus*). Simple, unforced, and carefully worded, the sonnet suggests that a good poem should be like a well-made wagon:

> I have made tales in verse, but this man made
> Waggons of elm to last a hundred years;
> The blacksmith forged the rims and iron gears,
> His was the magic that the wood obeyed.
>
> Each deft device that country wisdom bade,
> Of farmers' practice needed, he preserved.
> He wrought the subtle contours, straight and curved
> Only by eye, and instinct of the trade.
>
> No weakness, no offense in any part,
> It stood the strain in mired fields and roads
> In all a century's struggle for its bread;
> Beautiful always as a work of art,
> Bearing perhaps, eight thousand heavy loads,
> Homing the bride, the harvest, and men dead.

The wistfulness of the poem's first line betrays Masefield's fear that his work will not last as long as a well-made wagon. Without forcing the comparison, the sestet shows the wagon as a kind of living poem, seeing and bearing the full range of life while retaining the beauty that is necessary for a work of art.

Another fine sonnet, Shakespearean in form, is "Posted" (*The Wanderer*, 1930), Masefield's vision of the many wrecked ships lying unknown on the ocean's floor. He contrasts scenes of life above and below the water but dwells on the eerie particulars of the otherworldly environment beneath the waves:

> Dream after dream, I see the wrecks that lie
> Unknown of man, unmarked upon the charts,
> Known of the flat-fish with the withered eye,
> And seen by women in their aching hearts.
>
> World-wide the scattering is of those fair ships
> That trod the billow-tops till out of sight:
> The cuttle mumbles them with horney lips,
> The shells of the sea-insects crust them white.
>
> In silence and in dimness and in greenness,
> Among the indistinct and leathery leaves
> Of fruitless life they lie among the cleanness.
> Fish glide and flit, slow under-movement heaves.
>
> But no sound penetrates, not even the lunge
> Of live ships passing, nor the gannet's plunge.

In the first quatrain, the poet's sympathy lies above water level with the women and their aching hearts. The cold, withered eye of the flatfish is, in contrast, unfeeling and unappealing. This mood continues into the second quatrain, but in the sestet the undersea world begins to gain charm. It is fruitless, but it is also clean and quiet. Having nothing to do with the creatures of the air, it seems a peaceful resting place. Perhaps death at sea is not such a terrible fate.

Masefield generally avoided free verse, perhaps fearing that his work might sound unpoetic without rhyme. Rhyme often appears to be a crutch to him, an excuse to expand instead of a discipline to pare down. In his unrhymed poem "Liverpool, 1890" (*The Wanderer*) he picks his words with greater care than he often does when he is rhyming. Except for a trite last line, the poem is a most successful experiment for Masefield:

> Grey sea dim, smoke-blowing, hammer-racket, sirens
> Calling from ships, ear-breaking riveting, the calthrops
> Of great grey drays, fire-smiting on the cobbles,
>   dragging
> The bales of cotton.
>
> The warehouse roofs, wet-gleaming, the ships bedraggled,
> Awry-swung yards, backt on the main, the jib booms
> Run-in, the winches clanking, the slings of cargo
> Running up, jolt.
>
> There lie the ships, paint-rusted, each as a person
> In rake or sheer or rig, coulters and counters,
> Sea-shearing bows, those swords of beauty that thrust
> The heart with rapture.
>
> All fair ships, man-killers some, sea-eagles, sluggards.
> Tall, too, many: lofty, a dread to look at, dizzy thus:
> Among them always one more sky-aspiring queen,
> Remembered always.

The noisiness, the activity, the disorder of the docks comes across in the long lines, packed with hyphenated words. The catalogue of sights and sounds dizzies the reader. The introduction of the ships in the third stanza slows down the rhythm as Masefield lengthens his phrases and brings a focus to his randomly packed scene. The metaphor of the ship's mast piercing the heart with rapture strongly evokes the poet's long-standing passion for the beauty of sailing ships. Despite the disappointing last stanza, the poem is superior to the companion piece, "Liverpool, 1930," that follows it. In the latter poem, Masefield returns to a simple rhyme (*a b b a*) and slips into a distressing blandness.

Blandness is often a term used to describe Masefield's work as Poet Laureate. Undeniably, much of it is bland. However the weaker lines should not be allowed to obscure that portion of remarkably good work that Masefield produced between 1930 and 1967.

8

•••

Style and Reputation

The second half of the twentieth century has seen an explosion of literary criticism. Several hundred literary journals come out every year, and the size of the Modern Language Association's bibliography now approaches that of the Manhattan telephone directory. Today even the most obscure and unproductive writers are found out and written up. Amidst all this literary activity, one would expect someone of Masefield's stature to have attracted a good amount of attention. He has not. Aside from short biographical and bibliographical articles, nothing of substance on John Masefield's work has appeared in scholarly journals since 1930.[1]

Late in his life, Masefield good-naturedly alluded to his waning popularity by comparing himself to "a dodo or a great auk."[2] The metaphors were apt: although he had once been enormously popular, by 1960 his work seemed on the way to literary extinction. His career had begun auspiciously. The *Salt-Water Ballads* created a mild stir in 1902, and a decade later *The Everlasting Mercy* did considerably more. In the words of poet Robert Graves, it "set the Thames on fire,"[3] bringing Masefield a popularity that he enjoyed well into the 1930s. Between 1923 and 1930, over one hundred thousand copies of his *Collected Poems* were sold.[4] Interest in him lessened not because he lost his gifts, but because his style went out of fashion. What is remarkable is not his decline, but that he remained popular so long into the modern period, for Masefield was not a modernist poet.

The *Salt-Water Ballads* and *The Everlasting Mercy* seemed new when they appeared, but they still belonged to the Victorian tradition. Their directness, which sometimes bordered on the coarse, never obscured their moral core. Masefield's poems respected the feelings of the common man, the person whom readers had come to know so well in the Victorian novel. When modernism burst upon the literary scene at the close of World War I, it bore no resemblance to Masefield's work. T. S. Eliot's "The Love Song of J. Alfred Prufrock" was published only six years after *The Everlasting Mercy*, but Prufrock is worlds apart from Saul Kane. Intellectual, self-absorbed, and tentative, J. Alfred Prufrock exists in a fragmented and hopeless world. Neither philosophy, nor religion, nor any of the fruits of Western civilization offer him solace. His poem, like his world, is cut and pared down—not large, not full, not beautiful. Saul Kane is as open as Prufrock is closed, and the style of *The Everlasting Mercy* is as wild and lavish as its hero. No intellectual malaise disturbs Saul Kane's universe. He is too preoccupied with the physical life—drinking, cursing, and brawling in a noisy, vulgar world. He thinks sometimes, but not deeply. Masefield once said: "I don't think, I never could. . . . I just see or fail to see."[5] The same applies to Saul Kane. But in the end, Saul understands enough: God loves him and Jesus is his savior. *The Everlasting Mercy* closes with a harmonious vision of Saul Kane as a new Adam joyfully plowing the earth. No image could be farther from Eliot's *The Waste Land*.

Many critics have called Masefield a transitional figure, a bridge between the Victorian and the modern era. These attempts to update him do him a disservice, because his poetry is a failure if looked at through the modernist eye. Masefield may have been a contemporary of Yeats and Eliot, but he wrote more like Arnold and Kipling. He considered himself a Victorian poet and expressed little admiration for much of the work produced after World War I. "To the Victorians like myself," he said, "modern verse is without any inner life."⁶ His own work exhibits three general qualities that are at odds with modernism, but perfectly acceptable to the Victorian mind.

The first of these qualities is expansiveness. The reader is hard-pressed to find a Masefield poem that could be called chiseled or pared down. Even short lyrics like "Spanish Waters," seem fuller than they actually are by virtue of the piled-up phrases of description and the large number of syllables in each line. Masefield was a compiler, not a condenser. When he had not explained something well enough, he did not start over; he went on. The Victorian readers were accustomed to such writing. They loved long works and were happy to become lost in a multivolume novel or a book-length poem.

Although Masefield's works are often long, they are not inaccessible, and in this approachableness lies their second Victorian quality. Rather than alienating his readers, the length of Masefield's poems promised them detailed explanations and a world that was easy to enter. The often cryptic and intellectual utterances of the modernists spoke to a much more select group. Understanding "The Waste Land" demanded considerable effort, but anyone could sit down and read *Reynard the Fox*.

Because Masefield had the common touch, he was at his best when he wrote about the common man. He understood that adventure stories about simple people always move an audience. His lovers' quarrels, barroom brawls, and storm-tossed ships engaged his readers not only because of the element of fantasy inherent in them, but also because basic human emotions—fear, anger, jealousy—lay at their core. Masefield's contemporary audience felt the authenticity of his vision, and until two world wars jaded their hopes, they were uplifted by his positive outlook. It may be that Masefield was too popular, too accessible, and too easy to like. A reaction to his popularity was almost inevitable, abetted by a growing feeling that the world was more complicated than he chose to admit. T. S. Eliot spoke for the modernist generation when he said, "Poets in our civilization, as it exists at present, must be difficult."[7]

Masefield's poetry was decidedly not difficult. Its simplicity marks its third general characteristic. Uncomplicated diction, emotion, rhythm, and rhyme run through the greater part of Masefield's work. Where the modernist looked for the precise or unusual word or image to epitomize a difficult concept, Masefield sought the commonplace. We can see the difference if we compare Yeats and Masefield when they are writing on a similar theme—lack of fulfillment. In "Sailing to Byzantium," the beat of Yeats's lines is less regular than Masefield's and the stanzas are densely packed with unusual words and striking images:

> O sages standing in God's holy fire
> As in the gold mosaic of a wall,
> Come from the holy fire, perne in a gyre,
> And be the singing masters of my soul.
> Consume my heart away; sick with desire
> And fastened to a dying animal
> It knows not what it is; and gather me
> Into the artifice of eternity.

In contrast, Masefield's lines in the eleventh sonnet of *Animula* are more direct. Their beat is very regular and their imagery is built around a single metaphor:

> They say that as her husband lay a-dying
> He clamored for a chain to beat the hound.
> They say that all the garden rang with crying
> That came out of the air, out of the ground,
> Out of the waste that was his soul, may be,
> That had been kennelled in and now broke free
> Out to the moors where stags go, past control.

The result of the two different techniques is that Yeats appears to be musing on a knotty problem, while Masefield seems to be simply telling a story. Characteristically, Yeats uses the first person in his poem, unbothered by the implication that he is revealing something about himself. Masefield, on the other hand, carefully transfers the strong emotion into a third person, in an effort to remove himself from what he writes so feelingly about.

In keeping with the simplicity of his poems, Masefield professed to be a simple man, but he was not; he was enormously complicated. Said Audrey Napier-Smith ("Reyna"), "I always felt that he encased himself in a very thick shell (privacy or self-defence?) . . . and I felt he would never 'bare his soul' to anyone, except perhaps to his wife who was older than he and to whom he was devoted. Most of us have a 'threshold of secrecy' and guard it jealously and cannot talk about things we deeply feel about, and I believe his to have been a very broad one."[8] Because Masefield did not write openly about some of his deeper feelings, many tend to dismiss him as simpleminded. But the straightforwardness of his verse does not reflect a lack of appreciation of life's complexities; it expresses a wish for a world that is simpler and easier to live in than the one he saw. Out of context, the last line of "Biography"—"The days that make us happy make us wise"—seems naive. It is more complicated than that. It reflects a choice that Masefield has made, one that he explains in the preceding lines:

> Best trust the happy moments. What they gave
> Makes man less fearful of the certain grave
> And gives his work compassion and new eyes.

A positive attitude, according to Masefield, stimulates the poetic sensibility, giving the writer the advantage of understanding and perspective.

Although Masefield's simplicity, his expansiveness, and his accessibility were grounded in Victorianism, they were also derived from his lack of formal education. His work is totally without academic flavor. Interestingly, although he wrote over twenty-five volumes of nonfiction prose, not one (even the appreciation of Shakespeare) can be considered literary criticism. Masefield carefully avoided this peculiarly judgmental discipline. He had no love for criticism and no aptitude for it. Although he possessed considerable powers of observation and organization, he was less skillful when called upon to analyze and pass judgment. Overly sensitive himself, he was not inclined to publicly evaluate others. This does not mean that he had no opinions; privately he was quite willing to say what he thought. In a letter to Elizabeth Robins, he decried Sir Walter Scott's "horrible facility" and that "horrible fluent verse which so delights boys with its story and continual action."[9] Ironically, his own work was often faulted for these same excesses, and the reader wonders whether the practice of formal criticism might not have helped Masefield discipline his own writing.

Throughout his life, Masefield made light of his intellectual powers. His 1924 essay on Chaucer humbly begins with the disclaimer: "I am not learned and therefore do not know all the elements of Chaucer's mind." Two years before his death, he was still protesting his lack of intellectual gifts: "I am sorry to have to tell you that I am a very ignorant man, and do not know what men mean when they talk philosophy. I am a story writer, and am always drawn to narrative, seldom to drama or to pure thoughts."[10] Such modesty, however, did not indicate that Masefield thought himself inferior to intellectuals or critics. He is uncharacteristically vehement on the subject of critics in a letter to Florence Lamont:

To hear these critics, one would think that the diviner qualities of art were within the reach of all, for the taking. Let them try it. That may teach them a little humility; but they know better than to try it. They know it is a good deal easier to praise or blame than to understand.[11]

Masefield never differentiated between those critics who pontificate and those who carefully analyze and shed light on an author's work. To him, any sincere literary effort deserved praise. In such a spirit, he defended John Galsworthy against his attackers:

Galsworthy has written a great deal in the last twelve years. No man can always be at his best. You don't know what a strain writing is. You pour quarts of blood out each time. When a man is bled white for a while, you complain that the latest gush of blood isn't red enough. I say that it is blood of a jolly good vein, & interesting as such, even if it isn't as red as some.[12]

While defending Galsworthy, Masefield is answering criticisms about the uneven quality of his own work, too. His defense does not consider the writer's option of revision or of less frantic productivity as an antidote to literary anemia.

Modest as he appeared when speaking of his limitations, Masefield was nevertheless convinced that his own attitudes were the right ones. He belittled his lack of learning, but he could be quite dismissive of the intellectual's seemingly superior ability. In the Chaucer essay he explains pointedly:

If you are one sort of writer, you will now end [your story] by saying that the Cat killed the Rat. If you are another sort of writer, you will say that the Rat killed the Cat. If, on the other hand, you are neither, but only an intellectual, you will say they disagreed.

Intellectualism in twentieth-century poetry became associated with breaking from tradition, and this trend also ran counter to Masefield's background and sensibility. Because he was not formally educated, he deeply valued the lessons of the great writers whose works he had discovered without benefit of mentor or syllabus. The literary past was a treasure trove to Masefield, not a series of attitudes to react against. He learned an enormous amount from his homage to tradition — perhaps too much. It sometimes appears that an excessive regard for the past causes Masefield to stop listening to his own voice and his own experience. His dramas and poems lose their vigor when he abandons the common man for a mythical or historical hero. Although he himself had become famous and influential, Masefield could never really enter into the lives of the illustrious and the well-known in an imaginative way. Perhaps because he had been so vulnerable when he was poor and adrift himself, Masefield always portrayed the loner and the peasant with more insight than those whom fortune had favored.

As early as 1907, he expressed a desire to move away from the simple people, explaining to his publisher that "the old vein is worked out [and] one must expand one's range."[13] The "old vein" was probably not exhausted but too painful to mine all the time. Masefield sought distance as well as change as he moved from firsthand experience to stories that had already been told and characters who had been created by others.

The tug-of-war in Masefield's choice of subject matter also appears in his style. Just as the peasant often gave way to the potentate, so the rough and passionate style often yielded to one that was smoother and more restrained. All his literary life, Masefield struggled with an urge to become refined, to excise the rough and the unusual from his verse. In 1913 he described himself as "too young, too rebellious, and too coarse" to be named Poet Laureate — seeming to value these qualities — but he was just then basking in the success of *The Everlasting Mercy*.[14] In truth, he was not nearly so coarse as he pretended. Earlier, in the 1903 and the 1910 collections, and soon after in the 1914 sonnets, Masefield showed a tendency to regularize the beat of his lines and to speak in bland generalities. During these years, he alternated between a voice of ragged intensity and one of abstract refinement. As time passed, he began to favor the latter, for he was becoming prominent in the literary world. His popularity made him more conservative; people were listening to him, and he felt responsible for what he was telling them. Although he willingly accepted his position, he found the spotlight upsetting. Fame intruded on his privacy and the audience's curiosity about him helped to generate a public, patriotic Masefield persona.

Florence Lamont, in an early letter to the poet, inquired why so much poetry is sad. It was a deceptively simple question, one that Masefield responded to unguardedly:

[It is sad] probably because the world presses rather hard on sensitive people, & perhaps because men only take to poetry when something has unfitted them for action. But I really don't know. Perhaps no really deep feeling is really joyous.[15]

This note of personal melancholy rarely surfaces in Masefield's verse. He speaks generally, if at all, about how the world has "pressed" on him and about those experiences that have in some ways "unfitted" him for action. Only if one knows Masefield's story do certain of his themes and stylistic traits reveal his character. His aptitude for narrative and his difficulty with contemplative poetic forms like the sonnet underline his reticence and his desire to remove his poetry from his personal life. The frequent appearance of "lonely, hunted souls"[16] whose characters are strong and steadfast even in defeat also suggests Masefield's own early trials. Probably the most telling theme running through Masefield's work is his attachment to England. His preoccupation with English history, English pastimes, and especially with England as a seafaring nation demonstrates that, in a peculiar way, Masefield's native land took the place of the family he had lost as a child. Through his fame as a writer and his popularity with the English people, he regained the love and sense of family that were taken from him when his parents died. The more England rewarded him, the more devoted a native son Masefield became.

It is important to realize that the weaknesses of Masefield's style were apparent even when he was most popular: everyone knew that he sometimes went on too long, that his rhymes could be awkward, that he often waxed abstract and moralistic. It didn't matter. His work invited parody, but parody that was a compliment to him. In making fun of him, the parodists were acknowledging Masefield's ability to affect them. Whatever its faults, Masefield's work managed to move very large audiences for a quarter of a century. This was no mean accomplishment.

Just where Masefield's reputation is headed is difficult to say. The condescension of many modernists toward his work has led to its gradual disappearance from several anthologies of English poetry. However, as contemporary poets move away from the modernist aesthetic, Masefield's verse should become more appealing. At present, his tremendous output works to his disadvantage; a short volume of only his very best poetry could lure readers back into his world. It is a world worth entering—full of strong emotions, striking individuals, and a simple eloquence.

Notes

CHAPTER 1

1. Masefield to Robins, 10 January 1910, Masefield Papers, Berg Collection, New York Public Library, New York, NY.
2. Masefield to Robins, [Autobiographical Sketch for Elizabeth Robins], Berg Collection, [1910].
3. Ibid.
4. Ibid.
5. Constance Babington Smith, *John Masefield: A Life* (New York: Macmillan, 1978), p. 21.
6. Ibid., p. 29.
7. Quoted in Smith, p. 25.
8. Quoted in Smith, p. 32.
9. Ibid.
10. Quoted in Smith, p. 43.
11. Robins scholar Joanne Gates says there is no evidence Robins ever had an infant son that died. Conversation with June Dwyer, July 20, 1984.
12. Quoted in Smith, p. 127.
13. Peter Vansittart, ed., *John Masefield's Letters From the Front 1915–1917* (London: Constable, 1984).
14. According to Geoffrey Handley-Taylor, "Masefield did have several friendships via correspondence and occasional meetings with other ladies [than his wife] . . . going back as far as World War I. This was a delightful and quite innocent side of Masefield and these charming liaisons (totally innocent) he kept to *himself*." Letter to June Dwyer, 30 May 1985.
15. Masefield to Robins, [Autobiographical Sketch for Elizabeth Robins], Berg Collection, 1910.

CHAPTER 2

1. Masefield to Richards, April 21, 1908, Masefield Papers, Fales Library, New York University, New York, NY.
2. Quoted in Smith, p. 72.
3. Masefield to Richards, September 23, 1906, Fales Library.
4. Masefield to Richards, July 1, 1908, Fales Library.
5. There is no evidence that Masefield ever contemplated or attempted suicide. However, a letter to Elizabeth Robins contains a cryptic reference to it: "I will tell you another thing of mine. The taint of suicide. That was why I suffered so before Judith's birth." (January 12, 1910, Berg Collection.)
6. Smith, p. 85.
7. Masefield to Robins, February 10, 1910, Berg Collection.

CHAPTER 3

1. Frank Swinnerton, *The Georgian Literary Scene* (New York: Farrar & Rinehart, 1934), p. 209.
2. Quoted in Smith, p. 111.
3. Masefield to Robins, January 15, 1910, Berg Collection.

CHAPTER 4

1. *Times Literary Supplement*, October 5, 1911, p. 369.
2. *Times Literary Supplement*, June 18, 1908, p. 197.
3. Masefield to Robins, March 30, 1910, Berg Collection.
4. Masefield to Richards, undated letter, Fales Library.
5. Masefield to Robins, February 22, 1910, Berg Collection.
6. Girls probably read them, too. *Jim Davis* was dedicated to young Judith Masefield. She later remembered how her father read both *Jim Davis* and *Martin Hyde* aloud to her. See Corliss Lamont, *Remembering John Masefield* (Rutherford: Farleigh Dickinson University Press, 1971), p. 10.

CHAPTER 5

1. Smith, p. 121.

CHAPTER 6

1. Introduction to *Prose Plays* (New York: Macmillan, 1925), p. v.
2. Preface to *Prose Plays*, p. ix.
3. Introduction to *Verse Plays* (New York: Macmillan, 1925), p. v.
4. *Times Literary Supplement*, November 22, 1923.
5. Preface to *Prose Plays*, pp. x–xi.

CHAPTER 8

1. Arthur E. Dubois, "The Cult of Beauty: A Study of John Masefield," *PMLA* 45 (1930): 1218–57.
2. Quoted in Neil Corcoran's review, *Times Literary Supplement*, April 26, 1985, p. 469.
3. Lamont, *Remembering John Masefield*, p. 104.
4. Introduction to *Letters to Reyna*, ed. William Buchan (London: Buchan & Enright, 1983), p. 26.
5. *Letters of John Masefield to Florence Lamont*, ed. Corliss Lamont and Lansing Lamont (New York: Columbia University Press, 1979), p. 29.
6. *Letters to Reyna*, p. 47.
7. Quoted in Philip Larkin, *Required Writing* (New York: Farrar, Strauss, Giroux, 1982), p. 129.
8. "Reyna" to June Dwyer, June 9, 1985.
9. Masefield to Robins, March 23, 1910, Berg Collection.
10. Lamont, *Remembering John Masefield*, p. 99.
11. *Letters of John Masefield to Florence Lamont*, p. 82.
12. Ibid.
13. Masefield to Richards, April 16, 1907, Fales Library.

14. Quoted in Smith, p. 114.
15. *Letters of John Masefield to Florence Lamont*, p. 13.
16. G. Wilson Knight, "John Masefield: An Appreciation," in *John Masefield O.M.*, comp. Geoffrey Handley-Taylor (London: Cranbrook Tower Press, 1960), p. 11.

Selected Bibliography

The following is a chronological listing of Masefield's most important works. Unless otherwise stated, all books were published by William Heinemann in London and Macmillan Company in New York.

Salt-Water Ballads. London: Grant Richards, 1902.
Captain Margaret. London: Grant Richards, 1908.
The Tragedy of Nan and Other Plays. New York: Mitchell Kennerley, 1909.
The Everlasting Mercy. London: Sidgwick and Jackson, 1911; New York: Macmillan, 1912.
The Street of Today. London: J. M. Dent & Sons; New York: E. P. Dutton, 1911.
The Widow in the Bye Street. London: Sidgwick & Jackson; New York: Macmillan, 1912.
The Daffodil Fields. London and New York, 1913.
Dauber. London: William Heinemann, 1913.
Gallipoli. London and New York, 1916.
The Locked Chest; The Sweeps of '98. Letchworth: Garden City Press; New York: Macmillan, 1916.
Sonnets. New York: Macmillan, 1916.
Collected Poems and Plays. 2 vols. New York: Macmillan, 1918.
Reynard the Fox. London and New York, 1919.
Animula. London: The Chiswick Press, 1920.
Right Royal. London and New York, 1920.
Melloney Holtspur. London and New York, 1922.
Sard Harker. London and New York, 1924.
The Hawbucks. London and New York, 1929.
The Taking of the Gry. London and New York, 1934.
Victorious Troy: or The Hurrying Angel. London and New York, 1935.

A Letter from Pontus. London and New York, 1936.

Basilissa: A Tale of the Empress Theodora. London and New York, 1940.

Some Memories of W. B. Yeats. Dundrum: The Cuala Press; New York: Macmillan, 1940.

In the Mill. London and New York, 1941.

New Chum. London, 1944; New York, 1945.

On the Hill. London: William Heinemann, 1949.

So Long to Learn. London and New York, 1952.

In Glad Thanksgiving. London and New York, 1967.

Poems. New York: Macmillan, 1974.

Selected Poems. Ed. Donald Stanford. Manchester: Carcanet Press, 1984.

Collections of Masefield's Letters

Letters of John Masefield to Florence Lamont. Ed. Corliss Lamont and Lansing Lamont. New York: Columbia University Press, 1979.

Letters to Reyna. Ed. William Buchan. London: Buchan & Enright, 1983.

John Masefield's Letters from the Front 1915–1917. Ed. Peter Vansittart. London: Constable, 1984.

Letters to Margaret Bridges 1915–19. Ed. Donald Stanford. Manchester: Carcanet, 1984.

Selected Secondary Sources

Biggane, Cecil. *John Masefield: A Study.* Darby, Pennsylvania: Folcroft, 1980, reprint of 1924 ed.

Drew, Fraser. *John Masefield's England.* Rutherford, NJ: Fairleigh Dickinson University Press, 1973.

DuBois, Arthur E. "The Cult of Beauty: A Study of John Masefield," *PMLA* 45: 1218–57.

Hamilton, W. H. *John Masefield: A Critical Study.* Port Washington, NY: Kennikat Press, 1922.

Handley-Taylor, Geoffrey, compiler. *John Masefield O.M. A Bibliography and Eighty-first Birthday Tribute.* London: Cranbrook Tower Press, 1960.

Knight, G. Wilson. "Masefield and Spiritualism." In *Mansions of the Spirit*, ed. George A. Panichas, pp. 259–88. New York: Hawthorn Books, 1967.

Lamont, Corliss. *Remembering John Masefield*. Rutherford, NJ: Fairleigh Dickinson University Press, 1971.

Smith, Constance Babington. *John Masefield: A Life*. New York: Macmillan, 1978.

Spark, Muriel. *John Masefield*. London: Peter Nevill, 1953.

Sternlicht, Sanford. *John Masefield*. Boston: Twayne, 1977.

Thomas, Gilbert O. *John Masefield*. Darby, Pennsylvania: Folcroft, 1978, reprint of 1932 ed.

Wight, Crocker. *John Masefield, A Bibliographical Description of His First, Limited, Signed and Special Editions*. Boston: The Library of the Boston Athenaeum, 1986.

Williams, I. A. *Bibliography of John Masefield*. Belfast, Maine: Porter, 1979.

Copyright Acknowledgments

Index

117